PROBLEMS AND MATERIALS IN

EVIDENCE & TRIAL ADVOCACY

FOURTH EDITION

VOLUME TWO
PROBLEMS

ROBERT P. BURNS

STEVEN LUBET

THE NATIONAL INSTITUTE FOR TRIAL ADVOCACY

Adapted with permission and gratitude from materials
from the National Institute for Trial Advocacy (NITA) by James H. Seckinger

ISBN-55681-852-1
Burns, Robert P., and Steven Lubet, *Problems and Materials in Evidence & Trial Advocacy, Fourth Edition, Volume 2 Problems* (NITA, 2004).
7/04

PROBLEMS AND MATERIALS IN

EVIDENCE & TRIAL ADVOCACY

VOLUME TWO

PROBLEMS

Add abstraction to abstraction and one never reaches more than a heap of abstractions. But add insight to insight and one moves to mastery of all the eventualities and complications of a concrete situation.—Bernard J. F. Lonergan

VOLUME TWO

PROBLEMS

SUMMARY OF CONTENTS

PART ONE:
PROBLEMS, QUESTIONS, AND EXERCISES IN EVIDENCE

PART TWO:
PROBLEMS IN TRIAL ADVOCACY

PART ONE

EVIDENCE

PROBLEMS, QUESTIONS, AND EXERCISES

Contents

INTRODUCTION

These problems, questions, and exercises are based mainly on *State v. Mitchell* and *MacIntyre v. Easterfield*. (You will notice that the earlier problems are based mainly on *State v. Mitchell* and the later ones mainly on *MacIntyre v. Easterfield*.)

The problems contain different sorts of instructions. Most often you are asked to "argue" an issue. When you are asked to argue an issue, you should think through and be ready to present, in role, the best arguments for your designated side's point of view, as if you were arguing an objection at trial. The student presenting the objection to admissibility (the "opponent") should speak first, addressing the teacher as judge, and stating the objection(s). The student who is the "proponent" of the evidence should then respond to the objection(s). The opponent will then respond to the proponent's response. This portion of the class will be strictly "in role," but it won't take long for you to get the hang of it. The class will then consider the issues and questions that each argument raises. (It is usually possible to identify precisely what the issue is and what the relevant arguments are. The "answer" is sometimes more elusive.) Students must be present and prepared to present the arguments.

Working through these problems for yourself is a principal, perhaps the principal, way of actually learning the law of evidence. This requires doing the reading and thinking the problems through before class—something more active than just letting the class discussion roll over you. Note, too, that the topics are cumulative—you cannot understand hearsay unless you understand relevancy.

Sometimes you are asked to "consider" an issue. In those cases you are to think through the issues raised in light of the Rules and the Text and be prepared to discuss those issues.

Sometimes you are asked to perform a small segment of a witness examination. In those cases you are to ask precisely those questions you would ask the witness at trial on the topic indicated.

RELEVANCE

1. Read *State v. Mitchell* as a detective or historian might. Who did it? Why do you think so? (Several students may be assigned "adversary" roles as advocates to criticize the opinions and reasoning of our detectives/historians.)

2. Prosecutors tell a short (two-minute) story showing Brooke Thompson's deep affection for Leslie. Defense counsel tell a short (two-minute) story showing Brooke's indifference or hostility to Leslie. What makes one story more plausible than the other? [*Mitchell*]

3. Argue the relevance of the reduction of Brooke Thompson's income in October 1999, of the terms of the life insurance policy on Leslie, and the terms of the trust. Consider how relevance is related to theory of the case. [*Mitchell*]

4. Argue the relevance of Porter's hearing brakes screeching outside her window after 10 P.M. [*Mitchell*]

5. Consider the importance for the choice of prosecution theory of Joe's reaction to the news of his wife's shooting (page 14), agitation on the way to the station (page 16), of his excited insistence that 1751 Madison was not Leslie's home, and his statement, the substance of which was that Leslie should not have been at that address that night. [*Mitchell*]

6. Consider the relevance, under any theory of prosecution or defense, of the testimony that Leslie left her key on her bedroom table. What are you doing when you so consider?

7. Argue the relevance of Slyviak's observation of "a mark on the door post where the bullet might have struck and then dropped to the step . . ." (pages 13–14). [*Mitchell*]

8. Brooke Thompson offers "direct" (not circumstantial) evidence against Joe Mitchell. Are there any propositions, other than the propositions constituting the direct evidence, that you must believe in order to accept this "direct" evidence as true? If so, what reasons do you have for accepting those general propositions as true? What kinds of reasons are those? [*Mitchell*]

9. Assume for a moment that Chris Ravenna would testify that while Joe was in his shop, Sam went into the back of the store to get Joe's newly serviced revolver. As he was returning to the front of the store, he thought he caught a glimpse of Joe moving furtively away from a gun cabinet in which a number of .38 caliber revolvers were stored. An hour or two later he looked in that cabinet and noticed that a .38 on display was missing. He had checked it last the morning before, when he had found the .38 present. During the course of yesterday, there had been perhaps ten persons in the store, none of whom did he see near in the cabinet. Argue admissibility of the hypothetical testimony. [*Mitchell*]

10. Assume you are at a hearing on a motion to suppress Mitchell's statements made at the boarding house. The material fact presently at issue is whether a reasonable person in Mitchell's situation would have felt free to leave the officers' presence. Argue the relevance of Slyviak's testimony that the officers were instructed merely to "contact . . . Joe Mitchell, to inform him of the shooting and ask him to come to headquarters for further investigation. If he refuses, just leave." Prosecutors argue it is relevant; defense argues that it is not. [*Mitchell*]

11. In *MacIntyre*, argue the relevance of Jesse's attempts to borrow money in June and July 2002 (pages 21, 27).

12. Argue the relevance of Leslie's fear of Joe expressed to Quinn Washington, and Leslie's interpretation of Joe's letter of September 9, 2002 (pages 42, 73). Disregard hearsay issues. [*Mitchell*]

13. Consider the admissibility of the terms of the insurance policy that the Easterfields had on the missing brooch and their understanding as to the disposition of the proceeds. [*MacIntyre*]

14. Consider the relevance of such "background facts" as Joe's service in the Marines, Ross Easterfield's war record, Leslie Thompson's schooling and employment history. Such facts would normally be admitted simply to fill in the background of the story, though careful trial lawyers know how important they may be to some jurors. [*MacIntyre and Mitchell*]

15. Prosecutors argue the relevance of each of the pictures in the Mitchell file. Defense counsel argue the irrelevance of each of the pictures. What material proposition ("fact that is of consequence to the determination of the action") does each picture make more or less probable than it would be without the picture? Why? [You should be prepared to answer the equivalent questions for each problem in which relevance is at issue.] [*Mitchell*]-

16. Argue the relevance of Brooke Thompson's negative opinion of Joe if offered by the prosecution. Argue the relevance if offered by the defense. Put aside for now the opinion's admissibility under Rule 701. [*Mitchell*]

17. Argue the relevance of Joe's not stopping to say hello to Porter on his way up the stairs at 9:40–9:55 (page 48). Consider the relevance of Brooke's giving Leslie a ring on the night Leslie was shot (page 9). [*Mitchell*]

18. For each of the following pieces of evidence argue the relevance if offered by your side and the irrelevance if offered by your opponent: [*Mitchell*]

    a. The "first thought that flashed" through Brooke Thompson's mind after the shooting was that Joe had shot Leslie.

    b. Joe's drinking and blood alcohol level.

    c. Brooke's owning the .38 and its disappearance.

    d. Brooke's having seen Joe hundreds of times before at the same time and place.

19. Argue the relevance of Easterfield's encounter with Kelly Emerson at the time Kelly was eavesdropping outside the Easterfields' bedroom (pages 30, 51). Each side should argue its relevance for its case and its irrelevance for the other side's case. How can the same piece of evidence be arguably relevant for both sides? [*MacIntyre*]

20. Plaintiff in *MacIntyre* seeks to introduce Jesse's testimony concerning Ross Easterfield: "I had seen him jump up and shake a temporary maid who had spilled coffee on him at breakfast. He's a big man and he really shook her hard. I was afraid" (page 13). Argue relevancy. What if Jesse had included a claim for assault for Easterfield's threatening behavior in the library? Would the argument be easier? Why or why not?

21. Argue the relevance of the fact that Ross Easterfield is one of the richest men in the city. Argue the relevance of the fact that he is rumored to be one of the richest men. [*MacIntyre*]

22. Consider this: If questions of "logical relevance" are issues of logic and human experience and not of law, why should the judge be given the role of deciding them? If the doctrine of relevance exists mainly as a concession to the shortness of life, why not simply allocate time to the two sides and allow them to decide what is most relevant? In an adversary system, they should present the most relevant evidence, shouldn't they?

23. Consider this: If the judge in Mitchell makes every arguable (i.e., probably not reversible) relevance determination against you, will the jury see a "fair" picture of the evidence? [Mitchell]

24. Consider whether it would be more troubling if the "man who is telling the truth" letter (page 25) and the testimony with regard to Jerry Young (pages 16–17) were both excluded or if either one was excluded and the other admitted. If you think it would be more troubling, do the rules of evidence take into account your scruples about excluding both pieces of evidence? [Mitchell]

25. Argue the relevance of Brooke Thompson's racial attitudes. [Mitchell]

26. Argue the relevance of the fact that Ross Easterfield's club does not admit Catholics, Jews, or Blacks. [MacIntyre]

27. Argue the relevance of Brooke Thompson's landlording practices, including her willingness to take advantage of her relationship to her dead husband, the judge, for business purposes. [Mitchell]

28. Argue the relevance of Joe's membership in Men Angry About Divorce (page 29). [Mitchell]

29. Argue the relevance of Joe's barroom fight four years ago (page 27). [Mitchell]

30. Argue the relevance of Joe's shooting at the motorist (page 28). [Mitchell]

31. Argue the relevance of Mrs. Thompson's shooting in self-defense (page 5). [Mitchell]

32. Argue the relevance of the letter Slyviak describes (page 18). Consider Rule 104 issues. [Mitchell]

33. Jesse testifies on direct that she was not aware that Frank Holman planned to rob the gas station (pages 18–19). Consider the relevance of Frank Holman's having a criminal record at the time he attempted the armed robbery for which Jesse was imprisoned. Are there Rule 104 issues? [See pages 82–83.] [MacIntyre]

34. Argue the relevance of Brooke's statement to Leslie, "That man's a loser. I'd rather die than see you go back to him," and of Joe's "reaction" (page 9). Consider Rule 104 issues. [Mitchell]

35. Argue the relevance of Joe's walking toward the front door of the police station before he was arrested (pages 16, 34). Are there Rule 104 issues? [Mitchell]

36. Argue the relevance of Joe's aggravated assault case (page 28). Consider Rule 104 issues. [Mitchell]

37. Argue the relevance of the death of Joe's first wife (page 27). Are there Rule 104 issues? Assume for the moment that Joe had pled guilty to the shooting death of his first wife after a heated argument during their walk in the woods in Wisconsin and served eight years in prison. Now argue admissibility. [Mitchell]

38. Assume for the moment that Joe's grandparents left a will in which the family house was bequeathed to one of Joe's uncles. Joe was enraged that the house in which he grew up was left to someone else. After the reading of the will, he said to his uncle, "You've screwed me out of what is rightfully mine. If I can't have the house, no one will." Three days later the house mysteriously burned down. The police determined that the fire was set. Joe had an airtight alibi and their usual contacts did not yield any evidence Joe had paid someone to set the fire. Argue admissibility in this case. [Mitchell]

39. Defense offers to prove Joe's practice of listening to The Shadow regularly (pages 33, 48). Defense should conduct the segment of Joe's direct examination that would support admissibility (the "foundation"). Prosecution objects. Argue the legal relevance. [Mitchell]

40. Argue the relevance in *MacIntyre* of Jesse's placing money found around the house in the video cassette of Jesse James Rides Again.

41. Plaintiff in *MacIntyre* seeks to prove Mrs. Easterfield's "habit" of misplacing jewelry through the general testimony of Kelly Emerson (page 50). Any objection? Consider whether the plaintiff may ask Emerson to describe the incident recounted on pages 50–51 in order to prove the "habit."

42. Prosecution offers to prove through Chris Ravenna that Joe is a fast driver (page 53). Argue the relevance. [*Mitchell*]

43. Plaintiff in *MacIntyre* seeks to prove that the letter on page 93 was sent. Argue its logical relevance.

44. Easterfield denies receiving it. Taylor says that the church secretary sent the letter. Assume the secretary has no specific recollection of sending the letter. Consider whether the plaintiff is stuck. [*MacIntyre*]

45. Assume that Mr. Easterfield had a serious discussion with his wife in the presence of Kelly Emerson a week after Jesse left their employ. During that discussion he said, "From now on under no circumstances are you to discuss missing jewelry or anything else you cannot find with the house staff. No accusations . . . no questions . . . nothing. Come to me and me alone about such problems." Plaintiff offers to prove the conversation. Argue the objection. [*MacIntyre*]

46. Assume that Joe made bail while awaiting his trial. During the time he was out of jail (without telling his lawyer, who was not pleased) he began attending a weekly support group at a local community center called "Controlling Your Rage: Practical Techniques." Argue admissibility. [*Mitchell*]

47. In ultimately unsuccessful settlement negotiations in MacIntyre, the defendant's attorney said: "So, Easterfield despises your client and would like to see her suffer over this. That's why he contacted the loan company . . . So what?" Easterfield then made an offer of $30,000, which was rejected. Assume that Easterfield's lawyer has the authority to make admissions for him and there is thus no hearsay problem. Is the offer admissible as an admission of liability? Is the statement admissible if offered by the plaintiff to show malice? [*MacIntyre*]

48. Plaintiff seeks to inquire on Easterfield's cross-examination into his attempt to convince the Loan Company to prosecute Jesse criminally (page 31), contending that it provides evidence of malice, which is relevant both to the qualified immunity defense and to punitive damages. Defense objects under Rule 408, asserting that during settlement negotiations Easterfield offered to drop those efforts if she would accept $5,000 to dismiss the case. For the plaintiff, respond. [*MacIntyre*]

49. Plaintiff in *MacIntyre* seeks to admit the fact that the defendants have made no settlement offers at all. Argue the relevancy.

50. Assume that Jesse MacIntyre's criminal conviction is admissible under Rule 609. MacIntyre's lawyer argues that because Jesse pled guilty, the evidence is barred by Rule 410. For Easterfield, respond. [*MacIntyre*]

51. Consider the admissibility under Rule 411 of the insurance policy that Brooke had on Leslie (page 5). Assume that the homeowner's insurance policy that the Easterfields had in effect on July 17, 2002, excluded intentional torts. Defamation is an intentional tort. Consider the admissibility. [*Mitchell*]

52. Assume that the homeowners' policy does cover intentional torts, and Paul Pirro, the investigator who obtained the statement of Reeve Winsor (page 103), testifies that Winsor carefully went over the

statement to make sure it was accurate before signing it. Winsor tells a rather different story (page 57). Plaintiff seeks to reveal the existence of the liability policy on cross-examination of Pirro. Permissible? [MacIntyre]

53. In what ways does Rule 412 treat "character-type" evidence differently than do Rules 404 and 405? Is one approach superior to the other for all cases where a defendant offers to present evidence of a victim's character or past behavior? What is there about sex offense cases that justifies a different approach?

Rule 412 excludes evidence that a given defendant (whose defense is consent) may deem logically relevant under the very liberal standard of Rule 401. Could this exclusion result in the false conviction of some defendants? Are other rules of exclusion any different? If so, does that justify Rules 413–415?

Sexual offenses are dramatically under reported and some of the under reporting results from victims' fear of the public humiliation that the traditional rule permitted. Assume that many more perpetrators go unpunished than defendants could be falsely convicted because of the operation of Rule 412. Does that assumption justify the provisions of Rule 412? What kind of justification is appropriate? Do all evidentiary rules of exclusion rely on this kind of justification? If so, does that justify Rules 413–415?

54. Prosecution seeks to admit the results of the ballistics tests (page 80). Defendant seeks to admit only those results described in the first paragraph under "Ballistics Test." Argue admissibility. [Mitchell]

55. Prosecution seeks to admit the results of the skid mark tests (page 79). Defendant objects. Argue admissibility. [Mitchell]

56. Assume that evidence technicians found bloodstains on a jagged piece of metal on the fire escape leading up to Joe's room. A blood analysis showed it to be in the blood group A and to be Rh negative. Joe's blood belongs to that blood group and is Rh negative. Argue admissibility based on the following additional facts: [Mitchell]

   (1) Mr. Peter Sanguin, a biochemist, testifies. He testifies that 2 percent of the world's population is in group A, and about 10 percent have Rh negative blood. By the rule of compound probabilities, multiplying the two individual probabilities together allows one to determine the probability of the concurrence of the two variables. In this case it is under .25 percent. That means that fewer than 1 in 400 people have this concurrence. Argue admissibility.

   (2) Assume that the defense is aware of Dr. Sanguin's likely testimony. Before he is allowed to testify, the defense asks for a voir dire hearing outside the hearing of the jury to submit additional evidence. At the hearing, the defense proves the following facts:

      (a) A physical exam of Joe upon his arrest found no cuts or scrapes and Joe testifies that he was not on the fire escape and had no cuts or scrapes. Argue admissibility of Sanguin's testimony now.

      (b) A workman was on that fire escape on the afternoon of September 10. He remembers cutting himself on that same jagged piece of metal and

         (i) his blood type is A and Rh negative.

         (ii) his blood type is O and Rh negative.

   Consider admissibility of Sanguin's testimony assuming (a) and (b)(i) or (b)(ii).

(c)   A workman whose blood type is A and Rh negative was on the fire escape on September 10 but does not remember cutting himself. Consider admissibility of Sanguin's testimony assuming (a) and (c).

(d)   By an odd coincidence, three of the six people who live at Porter's have the concurrence of A and Rh negative. Consider admissibility of Sanguin's testimony assuming (1) and (3).

WRITINGS AND EXHIBITS

A. PHOTOS AND CHARTS

57. Argue the admissibility of the three photographs of the Easterfield home. [MacIntyre at 69–73]

58. Argue the admissibility of the four photographs of the Thompson front porch. [*Mitchell* at 63–71]

59. Argue the admissibility of the not-to-scale floor plan of the Easterfield home. [*MacIntyre* at 67]

60. Argue the admissibility of the not-to-scale diagram of the front of the Thompson home. [*Mitchell* at 57]

61. Argue the admissibility of the not-to-scale diagram of the streets around the Thompson home. [*Mitchell* at 55]

62. Argue the admissibility of the copy of the section map of Nita City containing annotations by the deputy city engineer. [*Mitchell* at 59–61]

B. REAL EVIDENCE

63. Argue the admissibility of the textbook *Modern Physics* by Henry P. MacIntyre. [*MacIntyre* at 52]

64. Argue the admissibility of the theater ticket taken from Joe Mitchell. [*Mitchell* at 75]

65. Argue the admissibility of the bullet recovered by Slyviak from the porch of the Thompson home. [*Mitchell* at 13–14, 75]

C. BUSINESS RECORDS AND PUBLIC RECORDS

66. Argue the admissibility of the certified copy of the Nita Transit Authority bus schedule. [*MacIntyre* at 75–76]

67. Argue the admissibility of the St. James Parish schedule of services. [*MacIntyre* at 77–78]

68. Argue the admissibility of the Certified Copy of the crime lab report. [*Mitchell* at 79–80]

69. Argue the admissibility of the coroner's report. [*Mitchell* at 81]

70. Argue the admissibility of Jesse MacIntyre's loan application. [*MacIntyre* at 85]

71. Argue the admissibility of Ross Easterfield's bank statement. [*MacIntyre* at 105–6]

72. Argue the admissibility of the ABC Employment Agency record. [*MacIntyre* at 115]

73. Argue the admissibility of Easterfield's desk calendar notes. [*MacIntyre* at 111]

D. LETTERS, ADS, ETC.

74. Argue the admissibility of the letter from Reverend Taylor to Ross Easterfield. [*MacIntyre* at 93]

75. Argue the admissibility of Joe's handwritten note to Leslie. [*Mitchell* at 73] Rather than introducing the letter may the prosecution simply ask Brooke Thompson what the letter said?

76. Argue the admissibility of the copy of the letter to Joe Mitchell from the Wilson Studios. [*Mitchell* at 23] Rather than introduce the letter, may the prosecution simply ask Slyviak what the letter said?

77. Argue the admissibility of the letter that purports to be from Jesse to Reverend Taylor. [*MacIntyre* at 91]

78. Argue the admissibility of the anonymous letter to the police department described by Officer Slyviak. [*Mitchell* at 25, 18]

79. Argue the admissibility of Nita Country Club ad from the *Nita City Tribune*. [*MacIntyre* at 123]

Rulings On Evidence

80. The following dialogue occurs on cross-examination of Joe in the trial court:

    Q.   Tell the jury how your first wife met her death.

    MR. JONES: OBJECTION.

    THE COURT: OVERRULED. ANSWER THE QUESTION.

    A.   She was shot in the chest by a rifle.

    Joe is convicted. May he raise the issue of the introduction of this evidence on appeal, based on the above dialogue? [Mitchell]

81. Defense counsel is cross-examining Brooke Thompson. She asks, "And what did you do with Leslie's possessions after her death?" The relevancy objection is sustained. Do what is necessary to preserve the error. [Mitchell]

82. The defense in Mitchell offers the letter on page 25. There is an objection based on inadequate authentication which is sustained. As if you were in the trial court, do what is necessary to preserve the issue of the letter's exclusion for appeal.

83. The prosecution in Mitchell calls an usher at the Palace Theater. He testifies without objection to Washington's words to Joe on the night Leslie was killed: "Joe, what have you done to Leslie? Why don't you leave her alone? She's afraid of you, Joe" (page 42). The prosecution then calls Ms. Washington and asks her what she said to Joe on the night of the killing. This time there is a hearsay objection which is overruled. Assume that the hearsay objection was valid. Consider whether the defense may obtain reversal predicated on the admission of Washington's testimony.

84. The prosecution in Mitchell finds and calls Maria Pietro (page 21). The defense objects, under Rules 404, 405, and 403, to the prior bad act evidence. The objections are overruled and Pietro testifies to her encounter with Joe as she did in his trial. Assume the objections were valid and were erroneously overruled. The defense then vigorously cross-examines Pietro and introduces extrinsic evidence that Pietro told the emergency room nurse that she was the aggressor and Joe acted in self-defense. The nurse remembers the incident well and is definite and credible. Pietro is not.

    Joe is convicted. May the defense obtain reversal predicated on the erroneous admission of Pietro's testimony? [Mitchell]

85. The appellate panel is considering the appeal under the circumstances described in problem 84. The panel reaches consensus on the truth of the following proposition: If we put aside the evidence of Joe's attack on Pietro, there is still adequate evidence independently sufficient to support the verdict. Should the panel hold that the trial court's ruling is harmless error? What if the panel determines that the evidence against Joe is "overwhelming"? [Mitchell]

86. Defendant in Mitchell seeks to elicit testimony from Brooke Thompson that she shot and killed one of her tenants. There is an objection as to relevancy and improper character evidence. When asked for his response, the proponent tells the court that the evidence is being introduced in order to show Brooke is a violent person. The objection is then sustained. Assume that, under the law of the jurisdiction, the evidence should have been

received to show Brooke's knowledge of the use of firearms. May the defendant urge the court's failure to receive the evidence as error on appeal?

87. The objection to the evidence in problem 86 is improperly overruled. Would the prosecution be able to urge that erroneous ruling as reversible error on appeal?

88. Jesse is on the stand. She seeks to testify that Kelly Emerson told her that she, Kelly, had just found the brooch in the library. Defendant objects that the evidence violates the Best Evidence Rule since Kelly would offer better evidence on the subject. The objection is erroneously sustained. The proper objection is hearsay, though the proponent might be able to lay a foundation for a present sense impression exception to the hearsay rule. May the proponent urge error on appeal? [*MacIntyre*]

89. Jesse's lawyers lose a motion in limine to exclude her school records, which are clearly inadmissible. However, they fail to object when those records are offered at trial, relying on the earlier ruling. May plaintiff urge error on appeal? (*MacIntyre*)

90. Jesse's lawyer objects to the introduction of her criminal conviction to impeach her under Rule 609. His objections are overruled. In closing argument, he argues extensively that Easterfield's accusations were especially cruel given Jesse's previous conviction and incarceration, justifying a higher award of punitive damages. Assume that the use of the conviction to impeach would be reversible error. May the plaintiff urge that error on appeal? [*MacIntyre*]

91. Make the same assumption as in problem 90, but assume that Jesse offers evidence only that she did not, in fact, know about Holman's intention to commit the robbery. May she urge the trial court's admission of the conviction as error? (*MacIntyre*)

92. The defense in *MacIntyre* offers lay opinion evidence that Jesse had a strong propensity to steal and manipulate her benefactors. The defense does not object, but seeks to offer evidence from a worker at the St. James Home that Jesse has often had the opportunity to steal while living and working there and has never taken a penny. Should the rebuttal evidence be permitted? [*MacIntyre*]

93. Slyviak is describing the trip from the boarding house to the station. He is asked, "What happened next?" Slyviak testifies, "Well, Joe said that he hoped that we wouldn't hold the shooting death of his first wife against him." What should defense do? Prosecution argues on appeal that whatever the defense did was untimely, since they did not object to the question. Respond. [*Mitchell*]

IMPEACHMENT

94. Consider the admissibility of Slyviak's testimony in *Mitchell* concerning his ability to see his partner from the porch of the Thompson home on September 10.

95. Argue the admissibility of Chris Ravenna's testimony in *Mitchell* concerning his ability to see Joe Mitchell as Joe left the gun shop on September 10 (page 52.

96. Mrs. Easterfield will not testify for the defendant in *MacIntyre*. Argue whether Kelly Emerson may testify that Mrs. Easterfield had an alcoholic beverage for breakfast on July 17 (page 33).

97. Mrs. Easterfield does testify. Argue whether she may be asked on cross-examination whether she had an alcoholic beverage for breakfast. If she denies having the drink, may Kelly Emerson testify that she did indeed have the drink? [*MacIntyre*]

98. Argue the admissibility of Reverend Taylor's testimony that Jesse called Kerry Easterfield "Isadore Easterfield" and her reaction to his inquiry as to where she had last seen the brooch (page 44). [*MacIntyre*]

99. In *Mitchell*, assume Raleigh Porter gives testimony favorable to Mitchell. Consider the admissibility of her having allowed Joe to fall behind on his rent while still living at the boarding house (page 45).

100. In *MacIntyre*, assume that Lee Marlow gives testimony favorable to Ross Easterfield. Argue the admissibility, on cross-examination, of Marlow's deposition testimony concerning the fate of the previous executive director of the club (page 63).

101. Reverend Taylor testifies for Jesse. Defendant seeks to cross-examine Reverend Taylor on the lunch with Jesse in order to show his bias in her favor (page 53). Defendant knows that Taylor and Jesse will deny any such meeting. Consider whether she may so inquire on the cross-examination of Taylor. If Taylor and Jesse deny the meeting, consider whether defendant may call Emerson to elicit her testimony on this matter. Are there Rule 104 issues? [*MacIntyre*]

102. Mrs. Easterfield has testified. On rebuttal, plaintiff recalls Kelly Emerson to testify that Mrs. Easterfield was thought by her house staff to be something of a liar (page 50). Argue admissibility. [*MacIntyre*]

103. The testimony in problem 102 is permitted. The defense seeks to cross-examine Emerson as to the incident Emerson described in her deposition in which Mrs. Easterfield took the blame for the botched dinner party (page 50). Argue the permissibility of the cross-examination. Assume Emerson cannot remember the incident. Assuming for the moment that the cross is permissible, how may the cross-examiner use the deposition transcript? Assume alternatively that Emerson denies that Mrs. Easterfield took the blame. May the defense cross-examine her as to whether she gave the description recorded on page 50? If she denies having said that at her deposition, what, if anything, may the defense do? [*MacIntyre*]

104. May Reverend Taylor testify that Jesse's reputation for honesty and veracity is good? If so, on cross-examination may the defendant ask Taylor about the incident in which the two twenty-dollar bills disappeared from the collection (page 46) and about her encounter with the T-Mart security official (page 20)? Argue the propriety of the cross-examination. [*MacIntyre*]

105. Mrs. Easterfield will testify for the defendant. Kelly Emerson says nothing about Mrs. Easterfield's veracity during Emerson's direct during the plaintiff's case. On cross, the defendant wishes to elicit Emerson's opinion that Mrs. Easterfield is a "truthful person" (page 50). Argue admissibility. [MacIntyre]

106. Kelly Emerson testifies for the plaintiff. On cross-examination the defendant wishes to question her concerning her statement to Mr. Easterfield that she had no knowledge of the fate of Easterfield's lobsters, a statement she admitted in her deposition to have been deceptive (page 51). Argue the permissibility of the impeachment. If she denies having deceived Easterfield, may she be impeached with the deposition statement? If she denies having made the statement in her deposition, may the court reporter be called to "complete the impeachment"? If the latter were permitted but the court reporter who recorded the deposition had no memory about what had been said, how could you complete the impeachment? (Assume, as is usual, the court reporter made and kept an audiotape cassette of the deposition and also took the deposition using the shorthand machine commonly used.) [MacIntyre]

107. Jesse testifies in plaintiff's case. On cross, no mention is made of the loan application on page 85. Plaintiff rests. Assume that the loan application on page 85 is properly authenticated and offered by defendant and that Jesse's statements on it are admissions of a party opponent and so not hearsay. There is a relevancy objection to the application and the judge asks the proponent what the relevancy is. He answers that it is offered to show Jesse's dishonesty since she has testified on direct that her income at the time she made the application was only $120 and that she did have debts at that time. Argue admissibility. Consider the applicability of Rules 608 and 613. [MacIntyre]

108. Is there any theory on which the loan application could be admitted? If there is, but the proponent relies on the "wrong" theory, will the opponent be able successfully to urge error on appeal?

109. Ross Easterfield has testified. Argue the admissibility of Winsor's testimony concerning Easterfield's reputation in the real estate world of Nita City ("a very aggressive deal-maker and a very hard, even slick, bargainer . . . Willing to conceal material information and even misrepresent facts") as described by Winsor (page 56). [MacIntyre]

110. Argue the logical and legal relevance in MacIntyre of Mrs. Easterfield's abortion offered by the plaintiff:

    (1) if Mrs. Easterfield has said nothing about the Easterfields' not having children on direct;

    (2) if Mrs. Easterfield has testified during her introductory testimony that "God hasn't blessed us" and

        (a) plaintiff seeks to cross-examine Mrs. Easterfield about the abortion;

        (b) after Mrs. Easterfield denies the abortion on cross, plaintiff seeks to call the doctor who performed the procedure; [Ignore privilege issues.]

        (c) without mentioning the abortion on the cross of Mrs. Easterfield, plaintiff calls the doctor who performed the procedure; [Again, ignore privilege issues.]

        (d) Mrs. Easterfield indignantly denies the abortion on cross and plaintiff recalls Jesse to impeach Mrs. Easterfield by testifying to the conversation between the Easterfields that she overheard (page 20);

        (e) plaintiff does not ask Mrs. Easterfield about the abortion on cross, but simply seeks to recall Jesse and to elicit the testimony from Jesse.

Assume you believe that all the impeaching "extrinsic" evidence (evidence that is not merely an admission on cross) is inadmissible, may you still ask Mrs. Easterfield about the abortion on cross, assuming, too, that you believe it is relevant? [*MacIntyre*]

111. Argue the admissibility on the cross of Easterfield of the contents of his talk at the real estate brokers' convention described on page 57. [*MacIntyre*]

112. Consider the admissibility of Winsor's testimony concerning the rumors about Easterfield's business practices in the small Ohio city he worked in before he came to Nita (page 56). [*MacIntyre*]

113. Chris Ravenna testifies that it is his opinion that Joe has a good character for truthfulness and should be trusted as a witness. May the prosecution cross-examine using any of the incidents described on pages 27 and 28 of the *Mitchell* file?

114. Assume that Easterfield is a witness in the case. Marlow testifies that Easterfield has the highest reputation for honesty, integrity, and fair dealing (page 64). On cross-examination, consider whether plaintiffs may question Marlow about any facts which they could not otherwise put before the jury. [*MacIntyre*]

115. Jesse testifies. May you confront her on cross-examination with the incident at the T-Mart? If she denies it, may you call the security guard? [*MacIntyre*]

116. Assume the impeachment of Reverend Taylor concerning the missing twenty-dollar bills is permitted and Taylor denies that entire incident occurred, may you impeach him with his deposition as a prior inconsistent statement? Assume the impeachment with the prior inconsistent statement is allowed, and Taylor denies saying that in his deposition. Defendant seeks to call the court reporter to impeach Taylor. For the plaintiff, make the objection. [*MacIntyre*]

117. Assume that the school record on page 121 is an official record and therefore, once authenticated, that it falls under an exception to the hearsay rule. Argue its admissibility offered by the defendant to prove that Jesse is "dishonest." [*MacIntyre*]

118. Argue the admissibility on Winsor's direct of testimony concerning the two successful civil suits against Easterfield. [*MacIntyre*]

119. Argue the admissibility on Winsor's direct of (1) Easterfield's criminal conviction described on pages 56–57, (2) the details of the crime to which he pled guilty, and (3) the circumstances surrounding the reception of the guilty plea. [*MacIntyre*]

120. In *Mitchell*, Porter testifies for Joe Mitchell. Argue the admissibility of her criminal conviction.

121. In *MacIntyre*, Marlow testifies that it was the settled policy of the club not to hire ex-convicts. Argue the admissibility on Marlow's cross of Reverend Taylor's conversation with Marlow described on pages 46–47. Consider Rule 104 issues. May the plaintiff examine Taylor concerning the conversation with Marlow without raising it on the cross-examination of Marlow?

122. Plaintiff in *MacIntyre* testifies that she was innocent of the attempted armed robbery with which she was charged. In rebuttal, defendant seeks to admit the stipulation of Mr. Johnson, MacIntyre's lawyer, recounted on page 80. Argue admissibility.

123. Jesse testifies consistently with her deposition as to the events of July 17. Defendants wish to impeach Jesse with the statement in her complaint, "On Sunday, July 19, Mr. Easterfield said within the hearing of Kelly Emerson, 'Miss MacIntyre has stolen a diamond brooch'" as they did in her deposition (pages 13–14). Is this tactically wise? Is this permissible impeachment? [*MacIntyre*]

124. Marlow testifies favorably for Easterfield. Marlow tells the jury the club has a long-standing policy prohibiting the hiring of ex-convicts. Pursuant to the policy, as soon as she learned that Jesse was an ex-convict she could not hire her. On cross-examination her attention is directed to the conversation with Reverend Taylor in which, according to Taylor, she seemed open to hiring of ex-convicts (pages 46–47). It is also suggested on cross that Marlow is afraid of Ross Easterfield and wants to please him. She denies Taylor's account of the conversation (page 63). Taylor then is allowed to testify to his conversation with Marlow concerning the club's willingness to hire ex-convicts (pages 46–47). On rebuttal, Marlow is recalled and seeks to testify to her statement to Mrs. Easterfield (page 63) that the club would never hire someone with a criminal record. Argue admissibility of the latter statement. [MacIntyre]

125. Reverend Taylor is the witness. Argue the admissibility of the conversation between Reverend Taylor and Ross Easterfield in which Easterfield told Taylor that he was not willing to employ another young woman from the St. James Home (page 44). For now, ignore privilege issues. [MacIntyre]

126. Assume that Ross Easterfield is asked on direct why he hired Jesse and he answers, "My only motive was pure Christian charity. No good deed goes unpunished, I guess." Now argue the admissibility of the conversation. [MacIntyre]

127. Argue the admissibility of Dr. Steinfels' opinion of Jesse's likely truthfulness as a witness (page 118). [MacIntyre]

128. Argue the admissibility of Dr. Steinfels' opinion of Jesse's likelihood to misperceive and misinterpret events (page 118). [MacIntyre]

129. Argue the admissibility of Dr. Steinfels' opinion of Jesse's propensity to steal (pages 117–118). Put aside any problems that stem from Steinfels' claim to be testifying as an expert. [MacIntyre]

PRIVILEGES

130. Ross Easterfield's real estate practices have led the local United States Attorney to prosecute him under the federal criminal RICO statute. Mr. Easterfield wants to prevent Mrs. Easterfield from testifying in the prosecution case, fearing that she is a "loose cannon." She is deeply offended at the prosecution of her husband and says she will not "take the Fifth." She wants to testify. The Easterfields cannot resolve their disagreement. May Ross Easterfield prevent his wife from testifying if the federal prosecutor calls her? [MacIntyre]

131. Easterfield and his attorneys have agreed that Mrs. Easterfield's testimony will, on balance, hurt Easterfield's cause. They wish to keep her from testifying if she is called as an adverse witness by the plaintiff and assert the marital testimonial incompetency by making a motion in limine. Assume this case is being tried in federal court and that the cause of action is a new federal statutory claim for civil penalties for defamation by employers. Consider whether the motion should be granted. Assume that this is a diversity action filed by Jesse after moving to California from Nita. Everyone agrees that the Nita law of defamation provides the rule of decision. What issues are implicated in deciding the motion? [MacIntyre]

132. The federal prosecution fails. The county prosecutor is embarrassed that the federal prosecutor filed his case before she did and files her own criminal case against Easterfield, based on a transaction not involved in the federal prosecution. Again, Easterfield does not want his wife to testify. If the state of Nita follows the rule in most state jurisdictions, what is the likely result? [MacIntyre]

133. The defense in *Mitchell* makes a motion in limine, seeking the exclusion of Leslie Thompson's exclamation, "Oh no . . . Oh no, Joe!" The defense does not at this point urge hearsay objections, but seeks to exclude the statement on grounds of the "marital testimonial incompetency." For the prosecution, respond to the motion.

134. The defense in *Mitchell* objects to the introduction of the letter on page 73 on the grounds of the privilege for marital communications. Argue the objection. Assume that Leslie and Joe were not separated, but that Leslie was merely staying with Brooke while her stepmother was recovering from surgery. Would the analysis be any different?

135. Assume that the plaintiff theory of the case relies in part on proving that the Easterfields' marriage was fragile. Argue the admissibility, if offered by the plaintiff through Kelly Emerson, of the heated exchange between the Easterfields on page 54. Now assume that the exchange took place at a time when the Easterfields reasonably believed that they were the only people in the house. Is the conversation admissible? [MacIntyre]

136. The plaintiff's theory of the case in *MacIntyre* is that, on July 17, the Easterfields were engaged in a knowing insurance fraud scheme to recover for the brooch which they themselves hid. The theory suggests that the Easterfields later decided that they did not want a thorough investigation and then placed the brooch where Emerson would find it. May the plaintiff question Mrs. Easterfield about conversations she may have had with her husband in which they allegedly planned the scheme? Argue the issue.

137. A month before her death Leslie was especially concerned about the threat of violence that Joe posed. She distrusted her judgment, however, about the seriousness of the danger. She asked her friend, Quinn Washington, to listen in on the other line of the telephone when she returned a call from Joe to her at the Thompson residence. During the phone conversation, Joe said these words: "I'm telling you straight out. I will kill you if you do not return to me." Argue the admissibility, through Washington, of the conversation. [*Mitchell*]

138. Jesse MacIntyre calls Mrs. Easterfield as an adverse witness. She wishes to ask Mrs. Easterfield the identical questions and get the identical answers contained in her deposition on pages 34–35. Argue the admissibility of the questions and answers put to Mrs. Easterfield before the first objection and instruction not to answer. Consider Federal Rule of Civil Procedure 32(b) and 32(d)(3) for purposes of making this argument. Consider Rule 104 issues based on the later deposition testimony concerning Emerson (page 80). [*MacIntyre*]

139. Joe Mitchell knows that Brooke Thompson sees a psychiatrist every two weeks. Mitchell recently received a phone call at the jail from the psychiatrist's office manager of many years, Joyce Bennington. She seemed very upset and said that she had seen the psychiatrist's notes for her last few sessions with Brooke Thompson. They seemed to indicate that the psychiatrist was helping Thompson "work through" her feelings of guilt for the killing of her stepdaughter. She said that she had always been loyal to her employer but that she couldn't "just idly stand by the blood of my neighbor." Argue the question of whether Mitchell may call the psychiatrist, subpoena the notes, or call the office manager to testify to the contents of the notes. [*Mitchell*]

140. The state is cross-examining Joe Mitchell. The State's Attorney asks Joe about the clothes he was wearing when he returned to his room on September 10. Joe's lawyer objects, "Objection, Your Honor, that topic was the subject of a confidential attorney-client communication from Mr. Mitchell to myself and I object on the basis of the attorney-client privilege." For the prosecution, respond. [*Mitchell*]

141. Joe Mitchell's lawyers received a call yesterday from Donald Weston. Weston is a semi-retired attorney at a major law firm. Weston said that he was consulted by a client last week and felt obliged to share with you the contents of that conversation. (He told you that he doesn't "give a damn" whether what he tells you is within the requirements of the attorney-client privilege or not.) His client is a prominent local psychiatrist who is treating Brooke Thompson. The psychiatrist told Weston that she was helping Brooke Thompson "work through" her feelings of guilt about her killing of her stepdaughter and wanted to know whether she had any legal exposure for failing to come forward with this information in order to save Mitchell. The psychiatrist told him that whether or not she had exposure she would never reveal what a patient told her, except, of course, within a conversation which was itself privileged such as his conversation with her attorney. Weston was unable to convince her to come forward. [*Mitchell*]

What issues are implicated in the question of whether Mitchell's attorneys may call and question the psychiatrist about what Brooke Thompson told her? May you call Weston himself (1) in lieu of calling the psychiatrist, or (2) in order to impeach the psychiatrist, should she be required to testify and deny that Thompson admitted the killing? [*Mitchell*]

142. Joe called his attorney at home at 10:15 P.M. on September 10. The attorney was out and his baby sitter took a message to call Joe at Mrs. Porter's. May the baby sitter be called simply to testify to Joe's attempt to talk with his lawyer? Argue the issue. [*Mitchell*]

143.   You represent Joe Mitchell, who is currently out on bail. He left your office at 2:30 P.M. on March 23. At 2:40 P.M., there was a hit-and-run accident a block away by a driver who resembled Mitchell. You have been subpoenaed to appear at a grand jury to testify as to whether Joe came to your office that day and the time at which he left. Is that information privileged? [*Mitchell*]

144.   Easterfield tells his lawyer to tell Jesse MacIntyre that he is sorry that he accused her in front of his wife in the library, to the ABC Employment Agency, and to Marlow. The next morning he calls his lawyer and tells him to forget it. [*MacIntyre*]

   Easterfield's lawyer receives the following Interrogatory:

   "Identify the time, place, and contents of all statements not privileged made by Ross Easterfield in which he describes in any way any statements made to the ABC Employment Agency and/or to Lee Marlow."

   Must Easterfield's lawyer identify the statement described in the first paragraph?

145.   Joe and his lawyer from his first trial were literally at one another's throats, with Joe physically attacking his attorney in anger over his "incompetence." The attack took place in the hallway outside one of the courtrooms. [*Mitchell*]

   Assume that Joe introduced opinion evidence in his second trial as to his character for peacefulness. May his first lawyer voluntarily come forward and offer to testify to his opinion as to Joe's violent character? May the state cross-examine Joe's character witness as to whether he took account of Joe's attacking his lawyer? May the state subpoena Joe's former lawyer to testify to (1) the attack, or (2) his (understandably quite low) opinion of Joe's peacefulness? [*Mitchell*]

146.   Reverend Taylor accompanied Jesse on her first visit to Jesse's lawyer and sat in on the first interview. Jesse says that Taylor "gave her the strength" to pursue her rights and that she could not have given the interview without him. The federal common law interpreted in light of reason and experience recognizes both a religious counselor and an attorney-client privilege. Argue the issue of the privileged nature of Jesse's statements and her attorney's statements in the initial interview. [*MacIntyre*]

147.   Jo Peterson is a member of your firm. She is the wife of Easterfield's second cousin and a good social friend of Easterfield's. She has always done Easterfield's personal tax returns. Peterson tells you after a few drinks that Easterfield came to her three days before his wife's brooch disappeared and asked for advice. Easterfield wanted to know whether insurance benefits for a "stolen" piece of jewelry were taxable. He also wanted to know whether any money made from the black market sale of a piece of jewelry falsely claimed to be stolen would be taxable. (Easterfield said that he didn't want to "screw around with the Feds.") Peterson answered those questions and told him to choose a very reliable fence for the resale. [*MacIntyre*]

   What ethical and evidentiary considerations does Peterson's revelation present?

148.   Assume that the *MacIntyre* case is a bench trial. Jesse's lawyer asserts that she believes that Easterfield had, with his lawyer's help, engaged in a knowing insurance fraud involving the brooch, and seeks to call Easterfield's trial counsel as a witness to show that.

   Assume you are Easterfield's counsel. You know that, in fact, Easterfield did ask a member of your firm about fencing the brooch, but that this firm member told him that this was wrong, that in no circumstances would she provide any advice on how to go about doing that, and

Easterfield was making a big mistake if he went forward.

Jesse's lawyer asks to inquire into the conversation between Easterfield and your firm member in order to determine whether that conversation was outside the privilege.

For Easterfield and your firm, respond.

149. Easterfield asks his lawyer to draw up leases of six months duration for one of his developments. You know that the local ordinance makes it a misdemeanor for a landlord to offer written leases of less than a year's duration. He does not seem to know that. Are Easterfield's communications with you on this subject privileged? [MacIntyre]

150. Assume that Officer Slyviak, when arriving at Joe Mitchell's room, saw on a table a half-written letter addressed to Mitchell's lawyer, which read: [Mitchell]

> Dear Attorney Pauline:
>
> I have done something terrible and I need your help. I shot and . . .

At this point the letter leaves off. Assume that as Slyviak moved toward the letter Joe said, (1) "That's not for your eyes!" (2) "Search anywhere you want. I have nothing to hide!" or (3) nothing. Under each of the three scenarios, is the letter privileged?

151. The prosecution wants to call the attorney who drew Leslie's will to testify to the virulence of Joe's hatred of Brooke Thompson exhibited by his statements in the interview he conducted with both Leslie and Joe present before she drafted the will. Argue the privilege question. [Mitchell]

152. Joe Mitchell's attorney received a telephone call three weeks ago. The person who called identified himself as Phil Jones and said that he was at the bar with Joe on the night of September 10. He said that he had read about Joe's situation in the paper and was sympathetic to Joe's plight. However, he told Joe's lawyer that he had some bad news. According to him, Joe said to him at the bar, "I have a problem and, by God, I am going to solve it tonight." Jones tells Mitchell's attorney that he intended to talk to the prosecutor about this. May Joe's attorney discourage Jones from speaking to the prosecutor? May or must Joe's attorney reveal the contents of the conversation to the prosecutor? [Mitchell]

A month later the prosecutor calls and tells Mitchell's lawyer that he received a phone call from a man who refused to identify himself who described the conversation recounted above. The prosecutor wishes to call the defense lawyer to testify to the identity of the person in the bar and to the contents of the conversation. Joe's statement is an admission of a party opponent and so not hearsay. If you can circumstantially authenticate the phone conversation and identify a hearsay exception for Jones' statement, may the prosecution call the defense attorney?

153. During the Easterfield trial Jesse's lawyer inquires into any conversations Marlow may have had with lawyers. Marlow responds that she had conversations with a lawyer at the same firm that represents Easterfield, and that she, Marlow, had gone to this lawyer for legal advice concerning her participation in this case. Marlow testifies that she had, in fact, received legal advice from this attorney. Jesse's lawyer asks her to tell the court the contents of the conversation. Any response to the privilege objections?

The judge overrules the objection. The testimony proves devastating to Easterfield's case. May Easterfield seek reversal based on an erroneous admission of the evidence?

154. You are Brooke Thompson's lawyer. Sadly, Brooke stepped in front of the 5:10 train three weeks ago in what the police thought was a suicide committed in grief over the death of her stepdaughter. You know different. She had confessed to you that she had killed Leslie herself but could not bear the anxiety over being discovered. The state intends to proceed with Joe's prosecution. (They have obtained a pretrial ruling admitting Brooke's identification of Joe as a statement of identification of a person.) [*Mitchell*]

Assume that you resolved your own ethical question in favor of informing Joe's attorney what you knew. Joe calls you as a witness.

For the state, make any objection. For the defense, respond.

155. Joe Mitchell wishes to call Frank Cato, a prominent criminal defense lawyer, who successfully represented Jerry Young in his criminal trials, to question him about anything Young may have told Cato concerning his actions on September 10. Assume that no one has seen Young for six months and, given the level of violence among his "business" associates, police think that he is dead. Argue the privilege issue. [*Mitchell*]

156. Mitchell calls Cato. Cato testifies, "Yes, I did have a conversation with Young concerning his whereabouts on September 10, but that is all I will say about the matter." By saying that much, has Cato waived the privilege? The judge finds that the privilege does not apply after making a preliminary finding that Young is dead, saying on the record that "I can't find that it's more probably true than not that he's dead, but there is evidence of Young's death sufficient to support a finding." The court orders Cato to testify further. Cato is as certain as he can be that the judge is wrong on the law. May he testify to Young's conversation? Must he testify to Young's conversation? If he does, has he waived the attorney-client privilege? [*Mitchell*]

He refuses to testify. What should the judge do? What should the defense do? What should Cato do?

157. Reverend Taylor testifies to Marlow's prior inconsistent statement described in Problem 125. Instead of calling Mrs. Easterfield, defendant wishes to call the partner in the law firm that advises the club on its corporate matters who will testify to a conversation with Marlow well before the MacIntyre matter arose in which Marlow asked the lawyer about the legality of a policy that excluded the hiring of ex-convicts. The partner advised her that such a policy was legal. Marlow then told him that they would follow such a policy. They then discussed the fact that the club had no Jewish, Catholic, or Black members. The partner advised Marlow that any policy of exclusion on religious grounds would violate the Nita statute. The law firm that serves as the club's legal advisor is the same firm that is representing Easterfield in the defense of MacIntyre's slander case. What issues are implicated in this situation? [*MacIntyre*]

158. Jesse asserts religious counselor privilege to protect the letter on page 91. Argue the issue. [*MacIntyre*]

159. Jesse asks Reverend Taylor concerning the conversation with Ross Easterfield on page 47. Easterfield asserts religious counselor privilege. Argue the motion. [*MacIntyre*]

PRESUMPTIONS AND BURDENS OF PROOF

160. At the end of all the evidence, Mitchell moves for a directed verdict ("judgment as a matter of law"). What standard will the judge employ in deciding whether to allow the case to go to the jury? Defendant makes the same motion in *MacIntyre*. Is the standard any different? [*MacIntyre* and *Mitchell*]

161. At the end of the prosecution case in *Mitchell* the judge concludes that no reasonable person could conclude beyond a reasonable doubt that Joe received the retraction letter from his publisher nor that he was trying to escape from custody at the police station. Must he or she direct a verdict of acquittal? For the prosecution, argue the directed verdict motion.

162. The Nita Criminal Code places the burden of proof, by a preponderance of the evidence, of sanity on the prosecution and the burden of going forward on the defense. Nita courts often say that Nita recognizes the "presumption of sanity." The prosecution puts on its case in *Mitchell* without any direct evidence of sanity. At the end of the prosecution case the defense moves to dismiss on the ground that the prosecution has not carried its burden of proving sanity by a preponderance. For the prosecutor, respond.

163. Jerry Young's widow has filed a civil action to require payment on his life insurance policy. Nita recognizes a presumption that a person is dead upon proof that he had disappeared from his home, was absent for a period of seven years during which time no tidings were received from him by his immediate family, and diligent efforts to establish his whereabouts were made and were unsuccessful. The death of the covered individual is an element in Mrs. Young's action against the insurance company. Nita has adopted Rules 301 and 302. How should the court direct the jury on the element of the death of the covered individual in each of the following situations: [*MacIntyre*]

    A.. Mrs. Young testifies that she is the only member of Young's immediate family, that he disappeared from their house nine years ago, and that she had not heard anything from him for all those nine years, and that she searched ceaselessly for Jerry. No evidence to the contrary is presented.

    B. Mrs. Young testifies as in A, but admits on cross that she did not attempt to contact members of any New York organized crime family to inquire as to Jerry's whereabouts. Given the large scope of Mrs. Young's other efforts, you do not believe that this omission would permit a reasonable juror to conclude that Mrs. Young's efforts had not been "diligent."

    C. Mrs. Young testifies as in A and B, but also testifies that she made no attempt to contact Jerry's cousins and aunts. You regard this omission as being sufficiently important to permit a reasonable juror to conclude that Mrs. Young's efforts were not "diligent."

    D. Mrs. Young testifies as in A. The defense calls George Watson, a man who was an acquaintance of Jerry's in Nita City. He testifies that while vacationing in Miami three years ago, he saw a man who "bore some resemblance to Young." He never approached the man, who was within his sight for perhaps five seconds. You regard this evidence as insufficient to permit a reasonable juror to conclude that Young is still alive.

    E. Mrs. Young testifies as in A. The insurance company calls Peg Parker who had met Jerry in Nita City once before he disappeared and whose son works for the defendant insurance company. Parker testifies that she met Jerry Young in a bar in Orlando three years ago. Parker had been engaged in small talk with this fellow for about fifteen minutes when Parker exclaimed, "You're Jerry Young, aren't you?" Parker's conversation partner smiled, winked, and said, "Keep a lid on it." He then left the bar. You regard this testimony as sufficient evidence to permit, though not require, a reasonable juror to find that Young is still alive.

F.   Mrs. Young testifies as in A and B, but also testifies that she received an unsigned handwritten letter four years ago which said only, "I will always love you." She testified that the handwriting "looked like Jerry's but I couldn't be sure." You regard this as evidence sufficient to permit, but not require, a reasonable juror to conclude that Mrs. Young received tidings from Jerry and/or that he is still alive.

Assume that Mrs. Young's action was a diversity action filed in federal district court in California. The federal court will apply Nita insurance law in deciding the case. California's version of the above presumption would shift the burden of proving that Young was still alive to the defendant and its conflicts law would apply its own version if the claim based on Nita law were being tried in a California state court. How should the court determine which law to apply? [MacIntyre]

164. Joe Mitchell is on trial. "Capital murder" in Nita requires that the state prove that the defendant specifically intended the death "of the person killed or another person." Relying on authoritative studies of the statistical relationships between higher caliber and lethal effect, the Nita legislature has enacted the following presumption: "A person who shoots and kills another person with a gun of caliber of .38 or higher shall be presumed to intend the death of the person killed." Nita also has enacted the following presumption, potentially applicable to Joe's letter from the Wilson Studios: "Any letter received and opened by a person shall be presumed to be read by that person." [Mitchell]

Nita has enacted Standard 303.

A.   Are Nita's presumptions constitutional in criminal cases?

B.   Slyviak testifies that the Wilson Studios letter was found open. Joe does not testify whether or not he read the Wilson Studios letter, and no other evidence is submitted. At the end of the case, the prosecutor asks that the court direct the jury to find that Joe had read the letter. How should the court rule? [Mitchell]

C.   At the end of all the evidence, putting aside the presumption, the judge is not convinced that a reasonable juror could find that Joe specifically intended to kill, rather than to wound or scare, his wife or Brooke. May the court submit the issue to the jury based on the force of the presumption? [Mitchell]

D.   How should the judge instruct the jury as to the effect of the presumption concerning the reading of mail? [Mitchell]

E.   How should the judge instruct the jury as to the effect of the presumption concerning intent to kill? [Mitchell]

165. Ross Easterfield is a very influential man. He has decided to seek legislative change to relieve the defendant of the burden of proving truth of a defamatory statement. His lawyers tell him that such a "merely procedural" change would control cases not yet tried. According to the bill that a friendly legislator is introducing for him, the plaintiff in a defamation action would have the burden of proving that the allegedly defamatory statement is untrue. Plaintiff and

defendant both send lawyers to the legislative committee considering the bill. Testimony before the legislative committee is limited to two minutes. Make your arguments for and against the change in the allocation of the burden of proof. [*MacIntyre*]

OPINION TESTIMONY

You should be prepared to argue whether each of the following is permissible testimony under Rules 602 and 701.

166.   Quinn Washington (page 42): "Joe seemed angry, especially when he spoke of Mrs. Thompson, and also nervous." [*Mitchell*]

167.   Pat Slyviak (page 16): "He [Mitchell] got very excited and said that 1751 Madison was not her home . . ." [*Mitchell*]

168.   Quinn Washington (page 42): "She [Leslie] said she had received a letter from him that day and that he made terrible threats against her and her mother in the letter. She seemed to be frightened of Joe." [Ignore, for the present, the hearsay problem of Quinn's reporting what Leslie said.] [*Mitchell*]

169.   Pat Slyviak (page 16): "As I exited our room I saw Mitchell walking very fast toward the front door of the station. He was looking around furtively like he was trying to sneak out. This was before we had told him he was under arrest. I'm sure he was making a run for it: you have a sense about these things after being on the street as long as I have." [*Mitchell*]

170.   Jesse MacIntyre (page 13): "From his words and appearance, I felt that he was accusing me of stealing the brooch. I couldn't believe what was happening and I was terribly hurt." [*MacIntyre*]

171.   Jesse MacIntyre: "Mr. Easterfield's country club is posh and lavish. The club is exclusive. It is only for the rich. The Easterfields treated me coldly. They always looked down on me. Mr. Easterfield was stiff and aloof. Mrs. Easterfield was careless about her jewelry." [*MacIntyre*]

172.   Brooke Thompson (page 8): "This man had a violent temper." [*Mitchell*]

173.   Brooke Thompson (pages 8–9): "Then he said to me: 'You are an evil person. You turned Leslie against me. You broke up this marriage, and I'll see that you pay for this. You'll be to blame for whatever happens now.' I cannot swear to the exact words used that night, but I do remember the substance of what each said." [*Mitchell*]

174.   Pat Slyviak (page 15): "I told him that we appreciated his cooperation. Mitchell acted voluntarily and on his own at all times. We never arrested him or demanded that he come to headquarters with us. He volunteered to do that." [*Mitchell*]

175.   Pat Slyviak (pages 13–14): "I recognized the bullet on the porch as a .38. On examining the door and doorway, I found a mark on the door post where the bullet might have struck and then dropped to the step where I picked it up. It might have passed through the victim's body and then struck the door post. Or it might have been dislodged from the victim's body by the impact of the fall." [*Mitchell*]

176.   Quinn Washington (page 41): "I'm sure if Mrs. Thompson objected to Leslie's marrying Joe, she did this out of a sense of conscience and duty to warn Leslie and to advise her for her own good." [*Mitchell*]

177.   Chris Ravenna (page 53): "I think she [Brooke Thompson] had such a hatred of Joe that, in her highly emotional state, she wanted to see Joe kill his wife. Her identification springs from her emotional bias toward him. She saw what her emotions wanted her to see." [*Mitchell*]

178. Jesse MacIntyre (page 15): "His words were so cutting and made me feel like I was the scum of the earth. I'll never forget what he said—he hurt me terribly then, and he's continuing to do it by making sure that I can't get a good job. He took away my self-respect and then he wouldn't even let me make a living. His words made me feel lower than I ever have since I left prison. It made me feel like when I was paraded in front of ordinary people in handcuffs . . . or when I had to submit to strip searches when returning from court to the prison." [*MacIntyre*]

179. Jesse MacIntyre (page 16): "When I talked to Marlow that day in the club, it looked like I would get the job for sure." [*MacIntyre*]

180. Jesse MacIntyre (page 18): "I've tried to get other jobs, at least ten or twenty, and nobody will hire me with Mr. Easterfield's bad character reference." [*MacIntyre*]

181. Pat Slyviak (page 16): "Yes, I did tell Bradley that my gut told me that Mitchell didn't do it. Frankly, I suspected the old lady but that's not the way the momentum of the investigation went and Bradley was calling the shots by then. I just think Mitchell was sincere about his having nothing to hide." [*Mitchell*]

182. Jesse MacIntyre (page 17): "Reverend Taylor became very angry. He's such a mild fellow. I've never seen him that angry before. 'I've always thought that Easterfield was a self-centered bas—, person. We'd have been better off if he hadn't gotten involved in this program at all. It's pure, thoughtless cruelty. A child pulling the wings off a butterfly. I'm just so sorry, Jesse.'" [Ignore the hearsay problem for now and consider only the admissibility of the various opinions expressed by MacIntyre and Taylor.] [*MacIntyre*]

Expert Testimony

183. Assume the bullet Slyviak recovered on the porch of the Thompson home was lost before it could be analyzed. Prosecution seeks to have Slyviak testify that the bullet was a .38 caliber bullet as on pages 13–14 of the file. Argue the issue. [*Mitchell*]

184. On the issue of damages, plaintiff seeks to elicit an opinion from Reverend Taylor that Easterfield's accusations were likely to be particularly painful for Jesse and were likely to make the process of her reintegration into society much more arduous. Plaintiff relies on Taylor's graduate degree in criminology and experience with former convicts. Argue the admissibility of the opinion. [*MacIntyre*]

185. Joe Mitchell seeks to call as an expert witness a psychologist who will (1) testify generally about the unreliability of eye witness testimony; will opine specifically that (2) Brooke Thompson's identification of Leslie's killer took place under circumstances that contained a particularly serious danger of error; and that (3) Brooke misidentified Leslie's killer. What would Joe have to establish in order to present the testimony? Which portions of the proposed testimony are most likely to be accepted? [*Mitchell*]

186. Joe Mitchell protested his innocence after he was arrested and offered to take a polygraph test. The detectives at the station obliged him and the test results were that he was telling the truth when he denied killing his wife. Joe wants to offer the results of the test. Whom should Joe call and how should he go about trying to admit the results? Is he likely to fare any better under the Daubert test than under the Frye test? [*Mitchell*]

187. The prosecution in Mitchell seeks to offer general evidence presented by a psychologist about a "stalker syndrome." The characteristics of the syndrome match Joe's behavior, but the psychologist would not draw any conclusions about this specific case. What would the proponent have to establish in order to admit the testimony? Would it matter that the psychologist testified further than Joe's behavior closely matched the characteristics of the syndrome? [*Mitchell*]

188. Taylor opines that Easterfield has done lasting psychological damage to Jesse and emphasizes the "devastating" effect of a "second" false accusation by someone in authority. Taylor is asked what he relied on in reaching this judgment. He testifies that he relied in part on the Order of the Prisoner Review Board (page 97), the Memorandum Opinion of the Attorney Registration and Discipline Commission disbarring Jesse's lawyer, and Mike Stiko's statement (page 95). The court has previously ruled that each of those is inadmissible under Rules 802 and 403 to show Jesse's actual innocence. For the plaintiff, lay the foundation to allow Taylor to describe that evidence. Argue admissibility. [*MacIntyre*]

189. Easterfield testifies that he was motivated by "pure Christian charity" in giving a job to Jesse and in all his dealings with her. After he describes his education and experience, Reverend Taylor is asked whether he has an opinion to the degree of certainty prevailing in the field of spiritual direction, as to (1) Easterfield's motivation in his dealings with Jesse, and (2) as to Easterfield's character for truthfulness. He seeks to share the opinion expressed on pages 43–44. Argue the objection. [*MacIntyre*]

190. Defense in *MacIntyre* calls Dr. Peter Steinfels (pages 117–118). After he testifies to his qualifications and the steps he took to form any opinion he has reached, the defense asks this question, "Doctor, were you able to reach a psychiatric diagnosis of Jesse MacIntyre?" Steinfels testifies that he has been able to reach a diagnosis. Defense then asks him what that diagnosis is. Argue the objections.

191.   Steinfels is permitted to explain the diagnosis described in the second paragraph of the letter (page 117). He is then asked whether he has an opinion, to the degree of certainty that prevails in the field of psychiatry, as to whether Jesse MacIntyre was lying when she was testifying in court. He replies that he has such an opinion and is asked to tell the jury his opinion. Argue the objection. [*MacIntyre*]

192.   Steinfels is then asked whether he has an opinion to the degree of certainty that prevails in the field of psychiatry as to whether Jesse accurately interpreted the events of July 17. He replies that he has such an opinion and is asked to tell the jury his opinion. Argue the objection. [*MacIntyre*]

193.   Steinfels is then asked whether he has an opinion to the degree of certainty that prevails in psychiatry as to whether Jesse attempted to steal the brooch. In fact, he believes that petty theft is a classic symptom of Borderline Personality Disorder and thus he has the opinion that Jesse tried to steal the brooch. He wishes so to testify. Argue the objection. [*MacIntyre*]

194.   After Steinfels gives his opinion as to Jesse's ability to interpret accurately the events of July 17, he is asked what he relied on in reaching his opinion. He replies that he relied on his observation of Jesse at her deposition and in court and on (1) the school record (page 121), (2) the uncharged shoplifting recounted by Jesse at page 18, and (3) the incident at the rectory in which the two twenty-dollar bills disappeared recounted at page 46. The court had previously ruled that those three pieces of evidence were inadmissible under, respectively, (1) Rule 802, (2) Rules 404, 403, and 609, and (3) Rule 104. For the defense, ask the foundation question(s) necessary to allow Steinfels to describe those three pieces of evidence. Argue the objection to Steinfels' describing the three pieces of evidence. [*MacIntyre*]

195.   Taylor testifies that he relied in part on the conversation he had with Easterfield, recounted on page 44, in reaching his opinion of Easterfield's character for truthfulness. He seeks to describe the conversation. Argue the objection. [*MacIntyre*]

HEARSAY

The next set of problems will deal with the rule against hearsay evidence and the exclusions from and exceptions to the rule. In each of the problems you must be prepared to address two questions. Is the "statement" hearsay? If it is, does it fall under any exception recognized by the Federal Rules? (Do not pass too quickly to the second question.) Where the instructions are to argue an issue you must consider whether you have an argument relating to each of those questions. If you do, you should prepare to present it. In some problems, you are instructed to lay the appropriate foundation, as if at trial, for the introduction of a "statement." You should in those cases prepare to ask precisely those questions which would warrant (provide the "foundation" for) the admissibility of the "statement." Be alert to authentication issues in phone conversations and to both authentication and best evidence problems with regard to documents.

196.   Prosecution seeks to admit Quinn Washington's testimony that Leslie Mitchell appeared "frightened and nervous." Defense objects that the "non-verbal conduct" of Leslie is hearsay. Respond for the prosecution. [*Mitchell*]

197.   Prosecution seeks to admit Slyviak's testimony that Joe was walking furtively toward the station house back door. Defense objects on hearsay grounds to the "non-verbal conduct" described. Respond for the prosecution. [*Mitchell*]

198.   Jesse seeks to testify that Emerson rolled her eyes after Mrs. Easterfield asked Jesse to go look for the brooch (page 11). Defense objects on hearsay grounds. Argue the objection. [*MacIntyre*]

199.   Kelly Emerson is asked to state her name for the court and the jury. Plaintiff objects on hearsay grounds and offers to conduct voir dire of the witness to show that she is relying on hearsay from her mother. Respond for the defense. [*MacIntyre*]

200.   Reverend Taylor seeks to testify that Mrs. Easterfield never complained about Jesse's demeanor or work. Argue the hearsay objection. [*MacIntyre*]

201.   Easterfield is testifying. He is describing the events of July 17 and says "I told her she could stay . . . " (page 26). Plaintiff objects and moves to strike as hearsay. For the defense, respond to the objection. [*MacIntyre*]

202.   Easterfield then testifies that Jesse responded "No!" to his invitation for her to stay (pages 26–27). Plaintiff moves to strike on hearsay grounds. Respond for the defense. [*MacIntyre*]

203.   Plaintiff in *MacIntyre* offers an edition of the Nita City Tribune containing the ad placed by the Nita Athletic Club (pages 59, 123). Defendant objects on hearsay grounds. For the plaintiff, respond.

204.   Plaintiff in *MacIntyre* calls Gina Lordowicz who owns a pawn shop in Nita. She seeks to testify that she was approached by a small-time thug whose name she doesn't know who told her "this Easterfield woman I know wants to unload a piece of jewelry off the books." Argue the hearsay objection.

205.   Taylor testifies consistently with his deposition as to Jesse's fine qualifications for the job at the club (page 46). Defendant seeks to introduce the letter he wrote to the Nita Transit Authority (page 99) to impeach his testimony. Argue the objection. [*MacIntyre*]

206.   Defense in *MacIntyre* calls Holman. Holman testifies that he told Jesse about his plans to rob the gas station before the attempted robbery. After his testimony, he returns to

San Diego to continue serving his prison term. In rebuttal, plaintiff seeks to introduce the statement on page 80. Argue the objection.

207. Emerson seeks to testify to the words the Easterfields exchanged in the argument recounted on page 54. Defendant objects on hearsay grounds. Argue the objection. [MacIntyre]

208. Marlow testifies for the defense. On cross-examination, the plaintiff seeks to inquire into the "rumor" that Marlow described on deposition about the firing of the previous executive director (page 63). Defendant objects on hearsay grounds. Argue the objection. [MacIntyre]

209. Plaintiff offers Reverend Taylor's letter on page 93. The only objection is hearsay. Respond to the objection for the plaintiff. [MacIntyre]

210. On redirect, Jesse is asked why she pled guilty. She answers she did that because her lawyer told her that if she didn't she would be found guilty anyway and sentenced to fifteen years (page 19). Defense objects and moves to strike on hearsay grounds. For the plaintiff, respond to the objection. [MacIntyre]

211. Jesse MacIntyre testifies that Marlow told her that she "is exceptionally well qualified for the job" (page 16). Defense objects and moves to strike on hearsay grounds. For the plaintiff, argue the objection. For the defense, respond. [MacIntyre]

212. Kelly Emerson is testifying for the plaintiff. She recounts her telephone call to Jesse after the brooch was found (page 53). She testifies that Jesse told her that "she [Jesse] couldn't get a job and that everywhere she turned Mr. Easterfield had ruined her chances for the job." Respond to the hearsay objection. [MacIntyre]

213. Reverend Taylor has testified. On cross, defense asks whether Jesse, on July 17, shouted out, "Do you think I took it [the brooch]?" and then started crying and said, "Oh, I'm sorry." Plaintiff objects on hearsay and relevancy grounds. For the defense, respond to the objection. [MacIntyre]

214. Ross Easterfield testifies for the defense. He seeks to testify to the conversation he had with Peter Zanoni on July 17 (page 28). Argue the hearsay objection. [MacIntyre]

215. Jesse testifies for the plaintiff. She seeks to testify that upon returning to the dining room on July 17, she said to Mrs. Easterfield, "You know it will turn up. It always does" (page 12). For the plaintiff, respond to the hearsay objection. [MacIntyre]

216. Plaintiff in MacIntyre calls Frank Holman. He proposes to testify that he did not tell Jesse about his plan to rob the grocery store. For the plaintiff, respond to the hearsay objection.

217. Plaintiff calls Kelly Emerson and questions her concerning Ross Easterfield's conversation with his wife concerning an earlier "missing" piece of jewelry. ("She looked down . . ." [pages 50–51].) Consider the admissibility of each of the sentences in Emerson's description of that exchange. [MacIntyre]

218. Ross Easterfield testifies for the defense. On cross-examination, the plaintiff asks him what Mrs. Easterfield said as Jesse left the library. ("That vulgar little tramp!" [page 26].) Argue the objection(s). [MacIntyre]

219. Ross Easterfield testifies for the defendant. During his direct examination, he testifies that he mailed the original of the letter on page 113 to the insurance company on July 21. (The insurance company has no record of receiving the original.) Defendant offers the printout of the letter. Argue any objection. [MacIntyre]

220. Marlow testifies for the defense. On cross-examination plaintiff seeks to inquire into Mrs. Easterfield's relationship with George Williams, the tennis coach (pages 62–63). She asks the following questions: [MacIntyre]

1. Was Mrs. Easterfield having an affair with your tennis coach?

2. Was there a rumor to the effect that Mrs. Easterfield was having an affair with your tennis coach?

3. [After laying the foundation for the conversation with George Williams recounted on pages 62–63.] What did you say to him and he say to you?

Argue the appropriate objections to each question.

221. Argue the admissibility of Jesse's statement, offered by her on direct, that Marlow's secretary called her on July 22 and: [MacIntyre]

1. asked her for her social security number,

2. described at length the employees' lounge at the club and told Jesse in detail how lavish it was, and

3. said, "I have already prepared your W-4 forms. They are here on my desk."

222. Quinn Washington is testifying for the prosecution. She testifies that, on the night of September 10, she said to Mitchell, "Joe, what have you done to Leslie? Why don't you leave her alone? She's afraid of you, Joe" (page 42). Defense objects on hearsay grounds and moves to strike. Argue admissibility of each of those sentences, one at a time, for the prosecution. For the defense, respond to the prosecution's arguments. [Mitchell]

223. Slyviak is testifying in the *Mitchell* case. On cross-examination defense asks whether Slyviak told Detective Bradley that Slyviak believed Mitchell didn't do it (page 6). The only objection is hearsay. For the defense, respond.

224. Jesse MacIntyre testifies for the plaintiff. She seeks to recount her conversation with the cab driver who took her to Reverend Taylor's and in particular the cab driver's remarks to her (page 15). Argue the objection. She then seeks to testify to what she told Marlow, recounted on the last twelve lines of the second full paragraph of page 17, beginning with, "You have a good job . . . " Argue any objection. [MacIntyre]

225. Reeve Winsor has been called by the plaintiff. During his testimony, he says that he negatively evaluated Jesse MacIntyre before he spoke with Ross Easterfield. Plaintiff seeks to confront him with his deposition testimony (page 55), "After I had spoken with Mr. Easterfield, I negatively evaluated her file . . ." Permissible? At the end of plaintiff's evidence, defense moves for a partial directed verdict, arguing that there is no evidence of causality between Easterfield's statements and the ABC Employment agency's negative evaluation. Ruling? [MacIntyre]

226. Marlow testifies that the club had a firm policy against the hiring of ex-convicts when Jesse applied. Reverend Taylor then seeks to testify that Marlow had previously offered to hire ex-convicts (pages 46–47). This alleged conversation had not been mentioned to Marlow on cross. Argue the objection. [MacIntyre]

227. Jesse testifies and is impeached under Rule 609 by her conviction in the Holman matter. On redirect, Jesse identifies her signature on her sworn statement (page 89) and offers the statement into evidence. Argue the objection. [MacIntyre]

228. Brooke Thompson testifies that she told the police officers who arrived at her home on September 10 that she had just seen Joe Mitchell kill her stepdaughter. Defense objects on hearsay grounds. Argue the objection. [*Mitchell*]

229. Pat Slyviak testifies that Brooke Thompson said when Slyviak arrived at the Thompson home that she had just seen Joe Mitchell kill her stepdaughter. Argue the objection. [*Mitchell*]

230. Defense in *MacIntyre* offers the (previously authenticated) loan application Jesse made to Fidelity (page 85). [See page 22 for Jesse's explanation.] Plaintiff objects on hearsay and relevancy grounds. Argue the objection.

231. Jesse has testified. On cross-examination, defense puts this question to Jesse: "Isn't it true that you testified at your deposition that Mr. Easterfield 'never seemed to take any of her [Mrs. Easterfield's] ravings seriously'?" Plaintiff objects on best evidence and hearsay grounds and on the grounds that the statement is improper lay witness opinion testimony. For the defense, respond. [*MacIntyre*]

232. Easterfield testifies that Jesse responded, "No!" to his invitation for her to stay (pages 26–27). Plaintiff moves to strike on hearsay grounds. Respond for the defense. [*MacIntyre*]

233. Jesse is testifying for the plaintiff. She testifies (page 15) that as she was leaving she said to Mr. Easterfield, "After all this time, now you're calling me a thief" and that they then said nothing. Argue the hearsay objection. [The defense knows that Mr. Easterfield would testify that he shook his head "No!" to Jesse's claim that he thought she was a thief (page 26). The defense also knows that Jesse would say that "Mr. Easterfield was shaking his head violently back and forth during this time." Should the court consider these two latter facts in ruling on admissibility? What procedure could the defense follow to allow the court to consider them?] [*MacIntyre*]

234. Jesse denies that she knew about Frank Holman's intention to rob the gas station. Defense calls the court reporter who took down the proceedings on page 80 and seeks to offer testimony to the "basis" there described. Plaintiff objects on hearsay grounds. Argue the objection. [*MacIntyre*]

235. Reverend Taylor is the witness. He seeks to testify that Kelly Emerson told him that breakfast was always served at the Easterfield house at 9 A.M. weekends and at 7 A.M. during the week. The only objection is hearsay. For the plaintiff, respond. [*MacIntyre*]

236. Joe has been charged with only one count, first degree murder. No conspiracy count is included. Prosecution offers testimony of the bartender at the Silver Dollar Bar that Ms. Porter's handyman, George Tomas, was in on September 13. The bartender would testify that Tomas mentioned that he had some extra cash to spend because he had been paid "a small bundle" to leave the ladder down on the fire escape at Porter's "a couple days ago. God knows why." Tomas died last winter. Argue the admissibility of Tomas's statement. [*Mitchell*]

Daniel Kiley is an old friend of Joe's with a long criminal record. Telephone records show he spoke with Joe on the phone two or three times after Joe was imprisoned. He would say only that he and Joe talked "small talk." Mrs. Porter would testify that Kiley telephoned her on September 26, identified himself, and said, "Joe wanted me to tell you that he had no intention of shooting Leslie, only 'the old lady.' You know why." Kiley denied calling Porter. Is Porter's proposed testimony admissible? [*Mitchell*]

237. The prosecution in *Mitchell* seeks to elicit from Chris Ravenna the following testimony (page 52): "I remembered I said to him [Joe] that he'd better be careful, because it was

loaded, or something like that." Ravenna would testify to saying that immediately after noticing two bullets in the gun, something that surprised Ravenna (page 52).

238. Kelly Emerson has testified only that she found the brooch "in the library." There was no cross-examination on that point. In the defense case, Kerry Easterfield testifies that Kelly Emerson told her that she found the brooch "hidden behind a book in the study . . ." (page 37). Argue the hearsay objection. [MacIntyre]

239. Assume Kelly Emerson described finding the brooch as she did in her deposition (page 52). In the defense case, Kerry now seeks to testify to what Kelly told her (page 37). Argue the objection. [MacIntyre]

240. Jesse seeks to testify (page 18), "In early August, Kelly Emerson called me and told me that the missing brooch had turned up in the library of the Easterfield home. She called me fifteen minutes after she found it, she said. I think that Kelly told me that Mrs. Easterfield admitted leaving the brooch in the library." Objection is hearsay. Argue the objection. [MacIntyre]]

241. Brooke Thompson testifies that she told the police officers who arrived at her home on September 10 that she had just seen Joe Mitchell kill her stepdaughter. Defense objects on hearsay grounds. Argue the objection. [Mitchell]

242. Pat Slyviak testifies that Brooke Thompson said when Slyviak arrived at the Thompson home that she had just seen Joe Mitchell kill her stepdaughter. Argue the objection. [Mitchell]

243. Jesse MacIntyre is testifying on direct. She testifies that Mrs. Easterfield, on the morning of July 17, asked her to look for the diamond brooch. She is then asked what she said in response ["All right, but I'd rather not. I have to go to church"]. Defense objects on hearsay grounds. Argue the objection. [MacIntyre]

244. Kelly testifies that she had a telephone conversation with Jesse after the brooch was found. In the conversation, Jesse said, "I just feel so, so bad. There's nothing for me, just nothing." Argue the hearsay objection. [MacIntyre]

245. Jesse seeks to testify that she said to Mr. Easterfield in the library on the 17th: "What's going on here? You're making me feel very uncomfortable" (page 12). Argue the hearsay objection. [MacIntyre]

246. Kelly Emerson testifies for the plaintiff. She testifies that Jesse told her, on the morning of July 17, "that she didn't want to be late that day, since the opening hymn was one of her favorites and always gave her the courage to go on" (page 51). Argue the hearsay objection. [MacIntyre]

247. Jesse testifies for the plaintiff. She seeks to testify to Reverend Taylor's remarks upon her return to the rectory on July 17: "I've always thought that Easterfield was a self-centered bas—, person. He'd be better off if he hadn't gotten involved in this program at all. It's pure, thoughtless cruelty. A child pulling the wings off a butterfly. I'm just so sorry, Jesse" (page 17). Argue the objection. [MacIntyre]

248. Jesse is testifying for the plaintiff. She testifies that when she arrived at Reverend Taylor's on July 17, she said that she "had left the Easterfields'" because Mr. Easterfield had accused her of stealing some of his wife's jewelry" (page 44–45). Argue the hearsay objection. [MacIntyre]

249. The objection is sustained. Jesse has now been cross-examined. The defense suggested on cross that Jesse left the house because she had been caught in the act of stealing and that the slander action was an idea hatched by a clever lawyer weeks later. On redirect, Jesse

again seeks to recount her words to Reverend Taylor. Now argue the objection. Consider whether it would matter whether Reverend Taylor was the witness to Jesse's words, rather than Jesse. [*MacIntyre*]

250. Kelly Emerson has testified that she cannot remember how she felt when Easterfield asked her about the brooch on the 17th and cannot remember whether Mr. Easterfield asked her how she herself felt about his inquiries on the morning of the 17th (page 52). Her recollection cannot be refreshed. Easterfield then testifies that he did indeed speak to Kelly several days after the 17th and "said something like 'Kelly, I hope you know that I did not mean to imply anything by asking you if you had seen the brooch on the morning Jesse left'" (page 27). Argue the hearsay objection. [*MacIntyre*]

251. The objection is overruled. Easterfield then testifies that Kelly replied, "No, of course not, Mr. Easterfield. I didn't feel that you were accusing me at all" (page 27). Again, there is a hearsay objection and motion to strike. Argue the objection. [*MacIntyre*]

252. Kerry Easterfield testifies for the defendant. She seeks to testify that she told her husband on the morning of July 17 that she remembered "thinking about the brooch when I was in the library for a few moments the night before, and how he had given it to me for our wedding, and that I was almost positive I went upstairs to our bedroom, took it off and put it on my dresser" (page 35). Objection? [*MacIntyre*]

253. Assume that Brooke Thompson's neighbor, John Samaritan, rushed over to her house after he heard the gunshot. Brooke told him that Joe had shot her with a revolver. Samaritan accompanied Leslie to the hospital in the ambulance. When the paramedic asked him what happened, Samaritan said, "Her husband shot her with a revolver." Assume the paramedic is called to give other occurrence witness testimony and is asked what Samaritan told him. The objection is hearsay. Response? [*Mitchell*]

254. Defense in *MacIntyre* wants Ross Easterfield's desk calendar to be physically in evidence as an exhibit. For the defense, ask Easterfield precisely the questions that would serve as a foundation. For the plaintiff, be prepared to object based on the foundation laid.

255. Ross Easterfield's bank statement was obtained from him in discovery. He received it in the mail from the bank. Does the hearsay rule preclude its admission? [*MacIntyre* at 105–106.]

256. Argue the admissibility of the St. James Parish Schedule of Services. [*MacIntyre* at 77–78.]

257. Winsor testifies for the plaintiff. For the plaintiff, ask precisely the questions necessary to admit the document at pages 115–116. For the defendant, make any objections, requests, and/or argument based on that foundation. [*MacIntyre*]

258. Defense in *MacIntyre* offers the (previously authenticated) loan application Jesse made to Fidelity (page 85). (See page 22 for Jesse's explanation.) Plaintiff objects on hearsay and relevancy grounds. Argue the objection.

259. An investigator for the plaintiff has reviewed all of the Nita City Athletic Club personnel records for the last twenty years. Over that period the club has employed approximately 1,214 persons. The investigator has subpoenaed the criminal records of each of those persons from the Nita City police. Eighteen of those employees were found to have had non-traffic criminal convictions by the time they were hired. Consider what the plaintiff would have to do to present the above information in a summary exhibit. [*MacIntyre*]

260. Marlow has testified to calling Reverend Taylor the day Jesse applied for the job at the club. The Rectory has a phonogram system on which a secretary records incoming calls. The

secretary would testify that, at the time of calls, she asks the name of each person who calls and records the call even if there is no message. The phonogram has no record of a call from Marlow on July 22. In rebuttal, plaintiff seeks to admit the phonogram records from July 22 showing no call from Marlow. Argue the objection. [*MacIntyre*]

261. Plaintiff offers the Nita Transit Authority Bus Schedule [*MacIntyre* at 75–76]. Respond to the hearsay objection.

262. Reverend Taylor is testifying. Plaintiff wishes to show that Jesse's attorney in the Holman matter was incompetent or worse. Taylor seeks to testify to reading the Memorandum Opinion of the Attorney Registration and Discipline Commission disbarring him for lack of zealous representation and that the Commission found that he had represented 600 criminal defendants between 1994 and 2001 and never tried a single one of their cases. All cases ended in plea bargains. Argue the objection. [*MacIntyre*]

263. Argue the admissibility of the certified copy of the Crime Lab Report. [*Mitchell* at 79–80.]

264. Argue the admissibility of the Coroner's Report. [*Mitchell* at 81.]

265. Argue the admissibility of the copy of the Section Map of Nita City containing annotations by the Deputy City Engineer. [*Mitchell* at 59–61.]

266. Defense in *MacIntyre* seeks to introduce a certified copy of Jesse's theft conviction to impeach her. Plaintiff objects on hearsay grounds. For the defense, respond.

267. Plaintiff in *MacIntyre* offers the certified copy of the Order of the Nita Prisoner Review Board (page 97). For the defense, state the objection. For the plaintiff, respond.

268. The cross-examination of Mrs. Easterfield suggested that she might have wanted to dispose of the brooch herself for cash. She indignantly protested that it was a beloved wedding gift and she would never part with it. She testifies further that she was married on June 7, 1982. Ross Easterfield has authenticated the Bill of Sale from Carol's as the Bill of Sale for the brooch. In rebuttal plaintiff seeks to introduce the Bill of Sale. Defense objects on hearsay grounds. Respond to the objection. [*MacIntyre*]

269. Peter Steinfels is on the stand. He has testified that Jesse MacIntyre suffers from Borderline Personality Disorder and that this mental illness makes it likely that she will misunderstand and misdescribe events occurring around her and that she will lie whenever it serves her interests. You know that you will call a psychiatrist, Greta Van Klimvitz, who will testify to the authoritativeness of Karl Kasper's text, General Psychopathology (1987). The latter contains the following sentences at page 40, "There is absolutely no evidence of any connection between diagnosed borderline personality disorder and misperception or prevarication. Indeed, borderlines are typically concrete and precise in their descriptions and honest even when social conventions would counsel some deception (socially acceptable 'white lies,' for example)."[*MacIntyre*]

On cross-examination, Steinfels is asked whether he considers Kasper's work authoritative in the field. Steinfels says it is an eccentric work and no reputable psychiatrist would rely on it. [*MacIntyre*]

For the cross-examiner, address the court in the manner that will allow you to invoke Kasper's opinion. Now do what you would do with the opinion?

Assume that you know that Steinfels will dismiss Kasper's work. Could you simply offer this segment of Kasper's text in your case in chief without bothering to ask Steinfels about it?

270. Mrs. Easterfield has testified. Plaintiff recalls Kelly Emerson to testify that Mrs. Easterfield's reputation for truthfulness is bad. For the plaintiff, respond to the hearsay objection. [*MacIntyre*]

271. The objection is sustained. Plaintiff wishes to call a law school classmate of Jesse's lawyer who will testify that Jesse's lawyer had a reputation at the local bar association for incompetence. Argue the objection. [*MacIntyre*]

272. Plaintiff calls his present cook, Vern Kosko, to testify that Jesse's general reputation in the community was not good: "She was viewed as a criminal type . . . you know what I mean." Argue the objection. [*MacIntyre*]

273. Consider the admissibility of Winsor's testimony concerning the rumors about Easterfield's business practices in the small Ohio city he worked in before he came to Nita (page 56). [*MacIntyre*]

274. Plaintiff in *MacIntyre* calls Frank Holman. He refuses to testify on the grounds that he might tend to incriminate himself. Plaintiff then seeks to introduce Holman's statement to the court (page 31). Argue the objection.

275. Plaintiff in *MacIntyre* reports to the court that Holman is in prison in San Diego and offers the statement on page 80. For the defense, respond.

276. Alice Adams lives in California. Defense seeks to offer the first question and the first answer from her deposition transcript (whose authenticity has been stipulated) recounted on page 82. Argue the hearsay objection. [*MacIntyre*]

277. The hearsay objection is overruled. For the plaintiff, urge the admission of the remaining questions and answers in the deposition. [*MacIntyre*]

278. Brooke Thompson testifies that her stepdaughter turned around on the porch of their home, looked out at the white car that had just pulled up, and then cried out, "'Oh no . . . oh no, Joe!' or something like that" (page 10). For the defense, argue admissibility. For the prosecution, respond. [*Mitchell*]

279. Plaintiff in *MacIntyre* has been unable to procure the attendance of Frank Holman at trial by subpoena. Plaintiff seeks to offer (through the court reporter) Holman's statement to the court (page 80). Argue the hearsay objection.

280. On the issue of damages, Jesse testifies that Marlow told her that tips at the club averaged $50 to $75 per week (page 15). Defense moves to strike on hearsay grounds. Argue the objection. [*MacIntyre*]

281. Marlow testifies for the defense. On cross-examination, Marlow is asked what the tips for hat check attendants averaged. Marlow says that they averaged $50 to $75 per week. Marlow is then asked how she knows that. She says that she knows it because previous hat check attendants told her that in the course of their negotiations on their base pay. She says that she always told them that it was only fair that she take into account their tips in determining their base pay. Defense now moves to strike the testimony. Argue the motion for the plaintiff. Oppose the motion for the defense. [*MacIntyre*]

282. Reverend Taylor is testifying for the plaintiff. Taylor seeks to testify that Jesse said that Marlow had said that a positive recommendation from Taylor would assure her the job at the club, regardless of anything else in her background (page 46). Argue the hearsay objection. [*MacIntyre*]

283.   Kelly Emerson testifies for the plaintiff. On cross-examination the defense seeks to elicit the following testimony (page 49): [MacIntyre]

> I recall that a cook who worked at the Easterfields for a few months, Martha Washington, told me that when Jesse had first seen the brooch, she had exclaimed, "My God, that's beautiful. I wish I had something half that gorgeous."
>
> I myself recall that Jesse told me once how "high class" the brooch was.
> I think she had a bit of a fixation on it.

Argue the objections to each of the sentences above.

284.   Reverend Taylor is testifying for the plaintiff. Taylor seeks to testify that Jesse said that she had learned from Marlow that Ross Easterfield accused her of stealing the brooch (page 47). Argue the hearsay objection. [MacIntyre]

285.   Jesse testifies for plaintiff (page 17): "I told Marlow then that, if Mr. Easterfield had accused me of theft while I was employed by him this was a lie. I told her that I had never stolen anything from the Easterfields. When I said this, Marlow looked down at the floor and was just silent." Argue admissibility of each of the first two sentences. [MacIntyre]

286.   Easterfield is permitted to testify to his alleged conversation with Mr. Zanoni (page 28). Plaintiff, in rebuttal, seeks to introduce the authenticated deposition transcript of Maria Zanoni (page 107). Argue the objection. [MacIntyre]

287.   Plaintiff in MacIntyre wishes to introduce Mike Stiko's sworn statement on page 95. Argue the objection.

288.   Marlow has testified for the defense. Marlow has testified that the club has always had a firm policy against the hiring of ex-convicts and that they never actually decided to hire Jesse before Marlow's conversation with Easterfield. In rebuttal, plaintiff offers to play the videotaped interview with Martha Van Kirk (page 125). Argue the objection. [MacIntyre]

JUDICIAL NOTICE

289. The court in *MacIntyre* takes judicial notice of the tightness of the job market for unskilled workers in Nita City, after the defendant presented the court with statistics from a current report of the Bureau of Labor Statistics showing the unemployment rate for unskilled workers to be 18 percent locally. The plaintiff objects that the numbers are not generally known and so are inappropriate to be judicially noticed. Ruling?

290. Assume that the plaintiff has a study conducted by two reputable economists at the University of Nita which criticized the methodology of the Bureau's study and concluded that the unemployment rate was only 8 percent. Assume further that the court has determined that the unemployment rate is relevant. What should the plaintiff do with the study? Under what conditions should the court take judicial notice of the unemployment rate? [*MacIntyre*]

291. Assume the court concludes that the Bureau's statistics are reliable and the study of the University economists is deeply flawed. It takes judicial notice. The plaintiff wishes to call the economists from the University to present their view of the unemployment rate. Should the court permit the contrary evidence? [*MacIntyre*]

292. The prosecution in *Mitchell* asks the court to take judicial notice that Marines receive training in firearms and that Joe Mitchell knew how to clean a gun quickly. Ruling?

293. Assume that the trial judge himself served in the Marines and knows that Marines receive training in the use of firearms. On that basis he is willing to take judicial notice. Permissible? [*Mitchell*]

294. Assume the trial judge is willing to take judicial notice that Marines receive training in the use of firearms. How should he instruct the jury on that question? [*Mitchell*]

295. Assume that it turns out to be necessary that the plaintiff in *MacIntyre* prove that the act of which Easterfield accused Jesse is a felony, something that requires that the brooch have a value of more than $1,000. Plaintiff rests without producing any evidence of the value of the brooch or of the criminal statute. The defense put on its case and moves for judgment as a matter of law at the end of all of the evidence, arguing that there is no evidence that the alleged act was a felony. What can the plaintiff do?

296. The court in *Mitchell* rules that Joe's aggravated assault incident is admissible under Rule 404(b) and that his acquittal does not preclude its admissibility in this case. The court takes judicial notice of the facts alleged in the indictment, concluding that he may notice "the contents of the documents in all the court files in this court system." Permissible?

CONCLUDING QUESTIONS

297. Is the law of evidence sufficiently definite to control the trial judge's discretion in deciding evidentiary questions?

298. Is the law of evidence sufficiently simple and clear that it can be used under the conditions that prevail in the trial courtroom?

299. As it applied in the *Mitchell* case and in the *MacIntyre* case, did the law of evidence further "the end that the truth may be ascertained and proceedings justly determined" (Fed. R. Evid. 102) or would it have frustrated those goals?

PART TWO

TRIAL ADVOCACY

PROBLEMS

CONTENTS

SECTION ONE—STORYTELLING

PROBLEM 1.   STORYTELLING   (*State v. Mitchell*)

Part One

A.   Describe the events of *State v. Mitchell* in the manner most favorable to the prosecution. Present your audience with the most important and persuasive information.

—Do not be concerned about the rules of evidence or trial formalities. You may structure your story however you wish, but it must be based on the facts and occurrences in the file.

—You will be limited to five minutes.

—In planning for this exercise, it will be helpful to consider:

•   What is the single most important point that you wish to convey?

•   What facts in the file make that point more likely to be believed?

•   Of these "supporting facts," which are the most important?

•   Which "supporting facts" are uncontested? Which are most subject to doubt?

•   How can the information be sequenced to make it more believable?

•   Are there any strongly negative facts for which you must account?

—Be prepared to discuss your choices and approach.

Part Two

A.   Describe the events of *State v. Mitchell* in the manner most favorable to the defense. Present your audience with the most important and persuasive information.

—Do not be concerned about the rules of evidence or trial formalities. You may structure your story however you wish, but it must be based on the facts and occurrences in the file.

—You will be limited to five minutes.

—In planning for this exercise, it will be helpful to consider:

•   What is the single most important point that you wish to convey?

•   What facts in the file make that point more likely to be believed?

•   Of these "supporting facts," which are the most important?

•   Which "supporting facts" are uncontested? Which are most subject to doubt?

•   How can the information be sequenced to make it more believable?

•   Are there any strongly negative facts for which you must account?

—Be prepared to discuss your choices and approach.

PROBLEM 2. STORYTELLING (*MacIntyre v. Easterfield*)

Part One

A. Describe the events of *MacIntyre v. Easterfield* in the manner most favorable to the plaintiff. Present your audience with the most important and persuasive information.

—Do not be concerned about the rules of evidence or trial formalities. You may structure your story however you wish, but it must be based on the facts and occurrences in the file.

—You will be limited to five minutes.

—In planning for this exercise, it will be helpful to consider:

• What is the single most important point that you wish to convey?

• What facts in the file make that point more likely to be believed?

• Of these "supporting facts," which are the most important?

• Which "supporting facts" are uncontested? Which are most subject to doubt?

• How can the information be sequenced to make it more believable?

• Are there any strongly negative facts for which you must account?

—Be prepared to discuss your choices and approach.

Part Two

A. Describe the events of *MacIntyre v. Easterfield* in the manner most favorable to the defendant. Present your audience with the most important and persuasive information.

—Do not be concerned about the rules of evidence or trial formalities. You may structure your story however you wish, but it must be based on the facts and occurrences in the file.

—You will be limited to five minutes.

—In planning for this exercise, it will be helpful to consider:

• What is the single most important point that you wish to convey?

• What facts in the file make that point more likely to be believed?

• Of these "supporting facts," which are the most important?

• Which "supporting facts" are uncontested? Which are most subject to doubt?

• How can the information be sequenced to make it more believable?

• Are there any strongly negative facts for which you must account?

—Be prepared to discuss your choices and approach.

SECTION TWO—BASIC AND DIRECT CROSS-EXAMINATION

PROBLEM 3.   BROOKE THOMPSON   (*State v. Mitchell*)

Part One

A.   For the prosecution, conduct a direct examination of Brooke Thompson.

B.   For the defense, conduct a cross-examination of Brooke Thompson.

C.   For the prosecution, conduct any necessary redirect.

Part Two

A.   For the prosecution, conduct a direct examination of Brooke Thompson limited to the events of September 10, 2002.

B.   For the defense, conduct a cross-examination of Brooke Thompson limited to the scope of the direct.

C.   For the prosecution, conduct any necessary redirect.

PROBLEM 4.   JOE MITCHELL   (*State v. Mitchell*)

Part One

A.   For the defense, conduct a direct examination of Joe Mitchell.

B.   For the prosecution, conduct a cross-examination of Joe Mitchell.

C.   For the defense, conduct any necessary redirect.

Part Two

A.   For the defense, conduct a direct examination of Joe Mitchell limited to the events of September 10, 2002.

B.   For the prosecution, conduct a cross-examination limited to the scope of the direct.

C.   For the defense, conduct any necessary redirect.

PROBLEM 5.   QUINN WASHINGTON   (*State v. Mitchell*)

A.   For the prosecution, conduct a direct examination of Quinn Washington.

B.   For the defense, conduct a cross-examination of Quinn Washington.

C.   For the prosecution, conduct any necessary redirect.

PROBLEM 6.   RALEIGH PORTER   (*State v. Mitchell*)

A.   For the defense, conduct a direct examination of Raleigh Porter.

B.   For the prosecution, conduct a cross-examination of Raleigh Porter.

C.   For the defense, conduct any necessary redirect.

PROBLEM 7.   OFFICER PAT SLYVIAK   (*State v. Mitchell*)

A.   For the prosecution, conduct a direct examination of Officer Pat Slyviak.

B.   For the defense, conduct a cross-examination of Officer Pat Slyviak.

C.   For the prosecution, conduct any necessary redirect.

PROBLEM 8.   CHRIS RAVENNA   (*State v. Mitchell*)

A.   For the defense, conduct a direct examination of Chris Ravenna.

B.   For the prosecution, conduct a cross-examination of Chris Ravenna.

C.   For the defense, conduct any necessary redirect.

PROBLEM 9.   JESSE MacINTYRE   (*MacIntyre v. Easterfield*)
Part One

A.   For the plaintiff, conduct a direct examination of Jesse MacIntyre.

B.   For the prosecution, conduct a cross-examination of Jesse MacIntyre.

C.   For the defense, conduct any necessary redirect.

Part Two:

A.   For the plaintiff, conduct a direct examination of Jesse MacIntyre limited to the events of July 17, 2002.

B.   For the prosecution, conduct a cross-examination of Jesse MacIntyre limited to the scope of the direct.

C.   For the defense, conduct any necessary redirect.

PROBLEM 10. ROSS EASTERFIELD   (*MacIntyre v. Easterfield*)
Part One

A.   For the defendant, conduct a direct examination of Ross Easterfield.

B.   For the plaintiff, conduct a cross-examination of Ross Easterfield.

C.   For the defendant, conduct any necessary redirect.

Part Two

A.   For the defendant, conduct a direct examination of Ross Easterfield limited to the events of July 17, 2002.

B.   For the plaintiff, conduct a cross-examination of Ross Easterfield limited to the scope of the direct.

C.   For the defendant, conduct any necessary redirect.

PROBLEM 11.   REVEREND MacKENZIE TAYLOR   (MacIntyre v. Easterfield)

A.   For the plaintiff, conduct a direct examination of Reverend MacKenzie Taylor.

B.   For the defendant, conduct a cross-examination of Reverend MacKenzie Taylor.

C.   For the plaintiff, conduct any necessary redirect.

PROBLEM 12.   KERRY EASTERFIELD   (MacIntyre v. Easterfield)

A.   For the defendant, conduct a direct examination of Kerry Easterfield.

B.   For the plaintiff, conduct a cross-examination of Kerry Easterfield.

C.   For the defendant, conduct any necessary redirect.

PROBLEM 13.   KELLY EMERSON   (MacIntyre v. Easterfield)

A.   For the plaintiff, conduct a direct examination of Kelly Emerson.

B.   For the defendant, conduct a cross-examination of Kelly Emerson.

C.   For the plaintiff, conduct any necessary redirect.

PROBLEM 14   LEE MARLOW.   (MacIntyre v. Easterfield)

A.   For the defendant, conduct a direct examination of Lee Marlow.

B.   For the plaintiff, conduct a cross-examination of Lee Marlow.

C.   For the defendant, conduct any necessary redirect.

PROBLEM 15.   REEVE WINSOR   (MacIntyre v. Easterfield)

A.   For the plaintiff, conduct a direct examination of Reeve Winsor.

B.   For the defendant, conduct a cross-examination of Reeve Winsor.

C.   For the plaintiff, conduct any necessary redirect.

Section Three—Introduction of Exhibits

GENERAL INSTRUCTIONS TO EXHIBIT PROBLEMS

Problems 16–33 all involve the introduction and use of exhibits.

For each problem you may offer the exhibit by calling any witness or witnesses you choose. You are not limited to the witnesses in the case files. Be prepared to respond to objections and to discuss your choice of witness(es).

You may oppose the offer by objecting and/or by conducting a limited voir dire examination. You need not object to an offer if there is not a reasonable basis on which to do so.

PROBLEM 16.   PHOTOGRAPHS OF EASTERFIELD HOME   (MacIntyre v. Easterfield)

A.   For the plaintiff, offer into evidence the photographs of the Easterfield home.

B.   For the defendant, oppose the offer (if feasible).

PROBLEM 17.   PHOTOGRAPHS OF THOMPSON FRONT PORCH   (State v. Mitchell)

A   For the prosecution, offer into evidence the photographs of the Thompson front porch (including photographs of the victim).

B.   For the defense, oppose the offer (if feasible).

PROBLEM 18.   Modern Physics by MacINTYRE   (MacIntyre v. Easterfield)

A.   For the defendant, offer into evidence the copy of Modern Physics from the Easterfield library. (You may create, if you wish, an exhibit that is consistent with the case file.)

B.   For the plaintiff, oppose the offer (if feasible).

PROBLEM 19.   CERTIFIED COPY OF BUS SCHEDULE   (MacIntyre v. Easterfield)

A.   For the plaintiff, offer into evidence the certified copy of the bus company schedule.

B.   For the defendant, oppose the offer (if feasible).

PROBLEM 20.   CERTIFIED COPIES OF CRIME LAB REPORTS   (State v. Mitchell)

A.   For the prosecution, offer into evidence the certified copies of the crime lab reports.

B.   For the defense, oppose the offer (if feasible).

PROBLEM 21.   MASS SCHEDULE   (MacIntyre v. Easterfield)

A.   For the plaintiff, offer the Mass schedule of the St. James Church for July 17.

B.   For the defendant, oppose the offer (if feasible).

PROBLEM 22.   EASTERFIELD'S BANK STATEMENT   (MacIntyre v. Easterfield)

A. For the plaintiff, offer into evidence Easterfield's bank statements.

B. For the defendant, oppose the offer (if feasible).

PROBLEM 23.   EASTERFIELD'S CALENDAR NOTES   (MacIntyre v. Easterfield)

A. For the defendant, offer into evidence Ross Easterfield's calendar notes.

B. For the plaintiff, oppose the offer (if feasible).

PROBLEM 24.   COPY OF LETTER FROM TAYLOR TO EASTERFIELD   (MacIntyre v. Easterfield

A. For the plaintiff, offer into evidence the copy of the letter from Reverend Taylor to Ross Easterfield.

B. For the defendant, oppose the offer (if feasible).

PROBLEM 25.   DIAGRAM OF EASTERFIELD HOUSE   (MacIntyre v. Easterfield)

A., For the plaintiff, offer into evidence the not-to-scale diagram/floor plan of the Easterfield home.

B. For the defendant, oppose the offer (if feasible).

PROBLEM 26.   DIAGRAM OF THOMPSON HOUSE   (State v. Mitchell)

A. For the prosecution, offer into evidence the not-to-scale diagram of the front of the Thompson home.

B. For the defense, oppose the offer (if feasible).

PROBLEM 27.   CITY MAP SEGMENT   (State v. Mitchell)

A. For the prosecution, offer into evidence the to-scale city map segment.

B. For the defense, oppose the offer (if feasible).

PROBLEM 28.   THEATER TICKET   (State v. Mitchell)

A. For the defense, offer into evidence the theater ticket recovered by the police in Mitchell's apartment. (Create an exhibit, if you wish.)

B. For the prosecution, oppose the offer (if feasible).

PROBLEM 29.   BULLET   (State v. Mitchell)

A. For the prosecution, offer the bullet recovered by the police. (Create an exhibit, if you wish.)

B. For the defense, oppose the offer (if feasible).

PROBLEM 30.   *Nita City Tribune* Ad   (*MacIntyre v. Easterfield*)

A.   For the plaintiff, offer into evidence the *Nita City Tribune* advertisement from the week of July 17.

B.   For the defendant, oppose the offer (if feasible).

PROBLEM 31.   ABC EMPLOYMENT RECORD   (*MacIntyre v. Easterfield*)

A.   For the plaintiff, offer into evidence the records of the ABC Employment Agency.

B.   For the defendant, oppose the offer (if feasible).

PROBLEM 32.   PURPORTED LETTER FROM JESSE MacINTYRE TO REVEREND TAYLOR
(*MacIntyre v. Easterfield*)

A.   For the defendant, offer into evidence the typewritten letter, purportedly from Jesse MacIntyre to Reverend Taylor.

B.   For the plaintiff, oppose the offer (if feasible).

PROBLEM 33.   BILL OF SALE   (*MacIntyre v. Easterfield*)

A.   For the plaintiff, offer into evidence the bill of sale for Mrs. Easterfield's brooch.

B.   For the defendant, oppose the offer (if feasible).

SECTION FOUR—CHARACTER EVIDENCE

PROBLEM 34.   ROSS EASTERFIELD   (MacIntyre v. Easterfield)

Assume that Ross Easterfield has testified on direct examination and that his testimony was consistent with his deposition.

B.   For the plaintiff, conduct a cross-examination of Ross Easterfield limited to the issues of character, bias, prejudice, and motive to fabricate.

C.   For the defendant, conduct any necessary redirect.

PROBLEM 35.   JESSE MacINTYRE   (MacIntyre v. Easterfield)

Assume that Jesse MacIntyre has testified on direct examination and that her testimony was consistent with her deposition.

A.   For the defendant, conduct a cross-examination of Jesse MacIntyre limited to the issues of character, bias, prejudice, and motive to fabricate.

B.   For the plaintiff, conduct any necessary redirect.

PROBLEM 36.   MacKENZIE TAYLOR   (MacIntyre v. Easterfield)

Assume that Reverend Taylor testified on direct examination and that the testimony was consistent with the deposition.

A.   For the defendant, conduct a cross-examination of Reverend Taylor limited to the issues of bias, prejudice, character, and motive to fabricate.

B.   For the plaintiff, conduct any necessary redirect.

PROBLEM 37   LEE MARLOW   (MacIntyre v. Easterfield)

Assume that Lee Marlow testified on direct examination and that the testimony was consistent with the deposition.

A.   For the plaintiff, conduct a cross-examination of Lee Marlow limited to the issues of bias, prejudice, character, and motive to fabricate.

B.   For the defendant, conduct any necessary redirect.

PROBLEM 38   BROOKE THOMPSON   (State v. Mitchell)

Assume that Brooke Thompson has testified on direct examination, and that her testimony was consistent with her earlier statements.

A.   For the defense, conduct a cross-examination that is limited to the issues of character, bias, prejudice, and motive to fabricate. [Note: Brooke's motive to commit the crime is not the subject of this exercise.]

B.   For the prosecution, conduct any necessary redirect.

PROBLEM 39   JOE MITCHELL   (*State v. Mitchell*)

Assume that Joe Mitchell has testified on direct examination, and that his testimony was consistent with his earlier statements.

   A.   For the prosecution, conduct a cross-examination that is limited to the issues of character, bias, prejudice, and motive to fabricate.

   B.   For the defense, conduct any necessary redirect.

SECTION FIVE—IMPEACHMENT

PROBLEM 40.   KELLY EMERSON   (MacIntyre v. Easterfield)

Assume that Kelly Emerson was called to testify for the plaintiff, and that her direct examination included the following:

`Mrs. Easterfield was always losing her jewelry and blaming other people. What upset me most was that even after the jewelry turned up, she never apologized to the people she'd chewed out. During the entire time I worked for her, I can't remember a single time that she said "I'm sorry, Kelly."

That's just the way she was. She used to blame her husband if they were late for parties, even though it was usually because it took her so long to get dressed and to put on her makeup. Once she blamed me for burning a roast, but the fact is that she'd sent me out to go marketing, and she said that she would finish cooking dinner herself. I wasn't even in the house when it happened, but she made me explain it to Mr. Easterfield. Thank goodness he was always so understanding.

On the day that Jesse was fired I saw Jesse and the Easterfields go into the library. It was my job to go out for the newspaper, and I stopped in the library to ask Mr. Easterfield whether he wanted the paper in the kitchen or the library. As I stuck my head into the room I heard Mr. Easterfield say "Jesse, I won't have a thief working for me." Jesse began to cry and I ducked back out of the room without saying anything. I don't think that any of them saw me, they were all so intent on each other.

A.   For the defendant, conduct a cross-examination on the basis of the above.

B.   For the plaintiff, conduct any necessary redirect.

[These materials are for the purpose of this problem only, and may not be used in the full trials of this case.]

PROBLEM 41.   KERRY EASTERFIELD   (MacIntyre v. Easterfield)

Assume that Kerry Easterfield was called to testify for the defendant, and that her direct examination included the following:

We've always had trouble with some of our help, but Mr. Easterfield and I have tried to do the best we can to give people a second chance. For example, I knew that Jesse MacIntyre was stealing loose money that we'd left lying around the house. Several times I saw her pick up a few dollar bills and slip them into a videotape in the library. I looked through the tape collection and found over $30 in the jacket for Jesse James. She never told me that she was doing this, and I certainly never gave her permission to do it.

On the morning of the brooch incident I originally sent Jesse upstairs to look for it. I stayed in the kitchen. I saw Jesse peek into the kitchen several times while I waited, but each time she saw that I was still in here and she left without saying anything.

I absolutely remember leaving the brooch on my dressing table that night. I know this because I recall that the clasp was stuck and I had to ask my husband to help take it off—I didn't want to damage my silk evening gown. Although I stopped in the library that night, Ross didn't. He went straight up to our bedroom, and I followed about ten minutes later.

I fired Kelly Emerson for stealing grocery money.

A. For the plaintiff, conduct a cross-examination on the basis of the above.

B. For the defendant, conduct any necessary redirect.

[These materials are for the purpose of this problem only, and may not be used in the full trials of this case.]

PROBLEM 42. REEVE WINSOR   (*MacIntyre v. Easterfield*)

Assume that Reeve Winsor was called to testify by the plaintiff, and that the direct examination included the following:

I did the background check on Ms. MacIntyre by calling her former employer, Ross Easterfield. I always keep the application that I'm working on in the typewriter while I'm conducting these reference checks, that way I know that I can type the person's comments directly onto the application. It's easier to keep track of things that way.

I know of Ross Easterfield from my earlier work in real estate. He has a fine reputation for truthfulness, and I didn't hesitate to take his word when he told me that he had fired Ms. MacIntyre. I didn't see any need to do any further checking once I had a negative evaluation based on reliable information from a man as prominent as Ross Easterfield.

You can imagine how surprised I was to learn that Mr. Easterfield was charging Jesse MacIntyre with theft. I remember that he was quite angry on the telephone. He kept using words like thief, criminal, and robber. I actually had to ask him to calm down so that we could finish the interview. He said that he would never consider using our agency for either his business or the Nita Country Club if we gave anything other than a "blackball" to Jesse MacIntyre. Those were his exact words.

A. For the defendant, conduct a cross-examination on the basis of the above.

B. For the plaintiff, conduct any necessary redirect.

[These materials are for the purpose of this problem only, and may not be used in the full trials of this case.]

PROBLEM 43. LEE MARLOW   (*MacIntyre v. Easterfield*)

Assume that Lee Marlow was called to testify by the defendant, and that her direct examination included the following:

Jesse MacIntyre seemed likeable enough when I interviewed her, but I wanted to give the process more time before I made any decisions. I had four or five more applicants already scheduled to come in, and I didn't want to make any decisions until I had seen them all. I explained this to Ms. MacIntyre and she seemed to understand.

I specifically informed her that we could not hire anyone with a criminal record. She seemed to understand what I was talking about, probably because we put that requirement in our ad for the position. Later, when I told her that she couldn't have the job, I explained that it was because of her criminal record. She got very angry and denied having a record. I think that a lie like that just confirms her bad character.

When I hired Martha Van Kirk I had no idea that she had a criminal record, if indeed she does. I didn't ask her, and she didn't say.

I have always been very happy with my job at the club. They've treated me fairly, and I've never had any complaints about salary, working conditions, or anything else.

A.   For the plaintiff, conduct a cross-examination on the basis of the above.

B.   For the defendant, conduct any necessary redirect.

[These materials are for the purpose of this problem only, and may not be used in the full trials of this case.]

PROBLEM 44.   JOE MITCHELL   (State v. Mitchell)

Assume that Joe Mitchell was called to testify for the defense, and that his direct examination included the following:

I am a peaceful man. I can almost always control my temper, and I would never think of violence as a good solution to a problem. Although Mrs. Thompson obviously hated me, I always tried to be understanding toward her. She was a lonely widow, and I understood that she saw me as a threat. Therefore, I tried to show her kindness and compassion.

When the police told me that Leslie had been shot, I insisted that they take me to the hospital. They refused, and said that I had to go to the police station first. That is why I agreed to go with them. I kept asking to go to the hospital until they told me that Leslie was dead.

A.   For the prosecution, conduct a cross-examination on the basis of the above.

B.   For the defense, conduct any necessary redirect.

[These materials are for the purpose of this problem only, and may not be used in the full trials of this case.]

PROBLEM 45.   BROOKE THOMPSON   (State v. Mitchell)

Assume that Brooke Thompson was called to testify for the prosecution, and that her testimony included the following:

I did my best to hide my negative feelings about Joe Mitchell. At least in the beginning, I tried to respect Leslie's feelings and to make my peace with the situation. So I kept my opinions to myself.

Joe Mitchell's car had a set of rubber dice hanging from the rear view mirror. Every time I saw them they reminded me of what a low-class bum he was. I saw those dice clearly on the night of September 10, when he drove up and shot Leslie. That's another way that I recognized his car.

I know of no one, other than Joe, who had any reason to harm me or my family.

A. For the defense, conduct a cross-examination on the basis of the above.

B. For the prosecution, conduct any necessary redirect.

[These materials are for the purpose of this problem only, and may not be used in the full trials of this case.]

SECTION SIX—ADVERSE EXAMINATION

PROBLEM 46.   ROSS EASTERFIELD   (*MacIntyre v. Easterfield*)

A.   For the plaintiff, conduct an adverse (direct) examination of Ross Easterfield.

B.   For the defense, conduct a cross-examination.

PROBLEM 47.   REVEREND MacKENZIE TAYLOR   (*MacIntyre v. Easterfield*)

Assume that the plaintiff rested her case without calling Reverend Taylor as a witness.

A.   For the defendant, conduct an adverse (direct) examination of Reverend Taylor.

B.   For the plaintiff, conduct a cross-examination.

PROBLEM 48.   LEE MARLOW   (*MacIntyre v. Easterfield*)

A.   For the plaintiff, conduct an adverse (direct) examination of Lee Marlow.

B.   For the defendant, conduct a cross-examination.

SECTION SEVEN—ADVANCED DIRECT AND CROSS-EXAMINATION

PROBLEM 49.   ROSS EASTERFIELD   (MacIntyre v. Easterfield)

For the defense, conduct a direct examination of Ross Easterfield limited to the discovery of the missing brooch and his subsequent actions.

A.   For the plaintiff, conduct a cross-examination.

B.   For the defendant, conduct any necessary redirect.

PROBLEM 50.   JESSE MacINTYRE   (MacIntyre v. Easterfield)

For the plaintiff, conduct a direct examination of Jesse MacIntyre limited to her background before working for the Easterfields.

A.   For the defendant, conduct a cross-examination.

B.   For the plaintiff, conduct any necessary redirect.

PROBLEM 51.   KELLY EASTERFIELD   (MacIntyre v. Easterfield)

Assume that Kelly Easterfield testified on direct, and that her testimony was consistent with her deposition.

A.   For the plaintiff, conduct a cross-examination on the question of Mrs. Easterfield's handling of her jewelry.

B.   For the defendant, conduct any necessary redirect.

PROBLEM 52.   JESSE MacINTYRE   (MacIntyre v. Easterfield)

Assume that Jesse MacIntyre testified on direct, and that her testimony was consistent with her deposition.

A.   For the defendant, conduct a cross-examination limited to the issue of damages.

B.   For the plaintiff, conduct any necessary redirect.

PROBLEM 53.   JOE MITCHELL   (State v. Mitchell)

For the defense, conduct a direct examination of Joe Mitchell limited to his relationship with Leslie.

A.   For the prosecution, conduct a cross-examination.

B.   For the defense, conduct any necessary redirect.

PROBLEM 54.   BROOK THOMPSON   (State v. Mitchell)

For the prosecution, conduct a direct examination of Brooke Thompson limited to her relationship with Joe Mitchell.

A.   For the defense, conduct a cross-examination.

B.   For the prosecution, conduct any necessary redirect.

SECTION EIGHT—EXPERT WITNESSES

The following materials are to be used for Problems 55 and 56. They may not be used for the full trials of *MacIntyre v. Easterfield*.

Assume that the court has ruled that the value of the Easterfield home is admissible on the issue of punitive damages.

PROBLEM 55.   GEORGE PETERS   (*MacIntyre v. Easterfield*)

A.   For the plaintiff, conduct a direct examination of George Peters.

B.   For the defendant, conduct a cross-examination.

C.   For the plaintiff, conduct any necessary redirect.

PROBLEM 56.   JOHN KRAUS   (*MacIntyre v. Easterfield*)

A.   For the defendant, conduct a direct examination of John Kraus.

B.   For the plaintiff, conduct a cross-examination.

C.   For the defendant, conduct any necessary redirect.

APPRAISAL OF REAL ESTATE

LOCATED AT

221 ROLLING HILLS LANE

NITA CITY, NITA

FOR

PETERS, GEORGE, AND LINTEL

AS OF

DECEMBER 18, 2002

DARIUS REALTY

One Central City Plaza   Nita City, Nita 56783   (231) 978-0906   DariusRealtyNita@NitaNet

December 20, 2002

Paulette Romney
PETERS, GEORGE & LINTEL
First National Bank Building - Suite 4565
114 Dearborn Street
Nita City, Nita 56784

Dear Ms. Romney:

At your request, I have examined the property located at 221 Rolling Hills Lane, Nita City, Nita and herein render to you my opinion of this property's fair market value as of December 18, 2002. The property is legally described as follows:

Lot 3 and the east 20 feet of Lot 4 in the Philips subdivision of Block 6 Williams and Jenkins subdivision of all that part of Section 9, township 24 north, range 14 east of the Fourth Principal Meridian, Darrow County Nita.

Market value can be described as the "highest price estimated in terms of money, which a property will bring if exposed for sale in the open market, allowing a reasonable time to find a purchaser who buys with the knowledge of all the uses to which it is adapted and for which it is capable of being used."

Attached to this letter you will find a report containing pertinent information and reasoning underlying my opinion.

I feel that as a result of the attached information, the fair market value of the property described herein, as of December 18, 2002, is estimated to be

ONE MILLION ONE HUNDRED AND FIFTY THOUSAND DOLLARS ($1,150,000).

Respectfully yours,

George Peters

DARIUS REALTY REPORT
Page 1 of 7

GENERAL INFORMATION

Location

Subject residence is located on the west side of Rolling Hills Lane, one block north of 47th Street, within the Garfield Park Highlands neighborhood of Nita City. The Garfield Park Highlands neighborhood is located on Nita City's northeast side, approximately five miles north and two and one-half miles east of the Central Downtown Business District of Nita City.

Transportation is available within walking distance via the Nita Commuter Railroad and the Nita City Transit Authority bus system. Excellent shopping facilities are located in the Garfield Plaza Shopping Center at 42nd and Peters. Schools are located within walking distance.

The immediate area is 100 percent improved, most homes range in age from 20 to 40 years and in value from $140,000 to $1,150,000.

SITE DATA

Shape:	Rectangular
Topography:	Rolling and sloping lot, wooded.
Frontage:	200 feet on Rolling Hills Lane
Depth:	420 feet
Area:	Approximately 84,000 square feet, or just under 2 acres
Paving:	Asphalt with a stone retaining wall border
Utilities:	Electricity, gas, water, and sewers
Zoning:	R-1, Single Family Homesite
Real Estate Taxes:	Approximately $27,500 paid in 2002, covering 2001 Taxes. Permanent Index No. 34-87-980–923.

DARIUS REALTY REPORT
Page 2 of 7

DESCRIPTION OF IMPROVEMENTS

Type:	Twelve Room Norman Style three story residence with basement, indoor swimming pool, and attached three car garage.
Construction:	Masonry
Age:	Main section of residence is 45 years old. Pool room, Florida room, and garage added in 1979.

Units and Rooms

Basement:	Laundry room, storage and boiler rooms, and a powder room.
First Floor:	Entrance and service halls, living room with cut stone fireplace to ceiling, dining room, kitchen, powder room, family room, Florida room, and pool room.
Second Floor:	Five bedrooms and three baths.
Third Floor:	Two bedrooms.

Construction Features

Foundation:	Poured concrete
Posts and Beams:	Steel
Walls:	Cut stone
Windows:	Most are metal casement type with upper portions of leaded glass and drop-in interior glass panels. Wood jalousi type in Florida room.
Roof:	Slate. Four skylights in pool room.
Gutters & Downspouts:	Copper

DARIUS REALTY REPORT
Page 3 of 7

Interior Finish

Floors: Ceramic tile at entry and in kitchen and Florida room. Others of oak. Oak parquet in living room and dining room.

Walls: Plaster, rosewood wall paneling and acoustical tile ceiling in family room. Wood tongue-and-groove paneling in pool room.

Kitchen: Ceramic tile floor, walls and ceiling covered with plastic tile, maple cabinets with butcher-block countertops (newer), double bowl stainless sink. Eight-burner Universal gas range with smoke-hood and exhaust fan: Butler's pantry.

Baths

Basement: Powder room, standard fixtures.

First Floor Powder Room: Ceramic tile floor and colored fixtures.

Second Floor: Three baths—all have ceramic tile floors and tubs with showerheads. Two baths have standard fixtures, ceramic tile wainscoting and glass tub enclosures. Bathroom in master bedroom appears to have 14-carat gold fixtures.

Mechanical and Equipment

Heating: Bryant, gas fired, multi-zone hot water boiler. Six fired infrared ceiling-hung heaters in pool room. Gas fired space heater in family room, two in pool room, a fourth unit with air conditioner in Florida room.

Hot Water: Two gas fired heaters, Sears, 120 gallon capacity and 75 gallon capacity.

Other: Wetbar in Florida room, newer electric service, sewers. Swimming pool: 20 feet x 40 feet concrete with filtering system and a gas water boiler, two exhaust fans.

DARIUS REALTY REPORT
Page 4 of 7

Miscellaneous

Fireplaces:	Living room
Site Improvements:	Attractive landscaping.
Garage:	Attached three-car with one double and one single overhead doors. Also a double overhead at rear of garage leading to a large concrete parking.
Patio:	Concrete, fenced rear yard, exterior floodlighting, stone barbecue grill.

Layout and Utility

Excellent

Condition

Very good, though owner indicated pool infrared lighting is inoperative.

Square Foot Calculations

Garage:	1,220 square feet	
Pool Room:	2,240 square feet	
1st Floor:	3,400 square feet	
2nd Floor:	3,220 square feet	
3rd Floor:	2,600 square feet	
TOTAL:		12,980 square feet

DARIUS REALTY REPORT
Page 5 of 7

VALUATION OF THE PROPERTY

In appraising the subject property, I have followed an orderly set of steps to reach a final conclusion of value. Both the cost approach and the market approach are included in my appraisal of the Easterfield property. Either of these methods can serve as an independent guide to property value. The separate estimates are correlated into a final opinion of market value, in which I have given the greater weight to the more relevant of these two approaches, the cost approach.

COST APPROACH TO VALUE

The cost approach is one of the steps in the valuation process. The indication of value derived from this approach is reached by estimating the value of the land and adding the cost of the improvements, less depreciation if any. The process falls into logical steps: estimating land value, making a careful inspection of the improvements to estimate construction cost while paying careful consideration to any possible economic or functional depreciation, and correlation of these estimates into an indication of value.

The building contains approximately 12,900 square feet.
Reproduction cost new 12,900 square feet at $170.00
per square foot: **$2,193,000.**

  Less: **Depreciation:**

      Physical   30 percent

      Economic 10 percent

      Functional <u>10 percent</u>

           50 percent   **<u>$1,096,500.</u>**

 Depreciated Cost of Improvements   **$1,096,500.**

  Add: **Land:**

      200 front feet at $1,000 per front foot   **$ 200,000.**

 Indicated Value by the Cost Approach   **$1,296,000.**

DARIUS REALTY REPORT
Page 6 of 7

MARKET DATA APPROACH TO VALUE

The market data approach for estimating the value of property is a process of comparing market data—that is to say, a comparison of the prices paid for similar properties, prices asked by owners, and offers made by prospective purchasers who are willing to buy. All of the properties referred to are in either a comparable area or the same general neighborhood as the property in question. All are within a one mile radius of the Easterfield property. It should be noted that market data is not being offered as independent evidence of the value of the property in question but only to validate and qualify the results of the cost approach.

No. 1.   **7899 N. Churchill, Nita City.** An eleven-room, five bedroom, three-bath, newer brick and stone, two-story residence on a smaller corner lot, reportedly sold in January, 2002 for $780,000. Subject property larger.

No. 2.   **3425 W. Arrowhead, Nita City.** A twelve-room, five-bedroom, four-bath, brick, two-story colonial on a lot 200 x 350 offered for sale in May of 2002 asking $990,000. No known offers.

No. 3.   **7889 Greenwood, Nita City.** A thirty-year-old, three-story Norman residence, eleven rooms, six bedrooms, four baths, on a lot with 100 foot frontage, reportedly sold in December, 2002 for $620,000. Subject property larger in size and on a large lot.

No. 4.   **4556 N. Dodson, Nita City.** A seven-year-old brick and stone colonial residence, Ten rooms, six bedrooms, five baths on a lot 120 x 200 feet, reportedly sold in April of 2001 for $720,000.

No. 5.   **389 Rolling Hills Lane, Nita City.** An older Norman style residence, three story, twelve rooms, six bedrooms, three-and-a-half baths, on a lot 200 ft. x 150 ft., taxes $24,040. Offered for sale in November, 2002, asking $820,000. No known offers.

No. 6.   **5134 N. Dodson, Nita City.** A stone, three-story residence, thirteen rooms, seven bedrooms, three-and-a-half baths, on a lot 350 ft. x 200, Year 2000 taxes $27,000. Reportedly sold in January, 2002 for $740,000.

DARIUS REALTY REPORT
Page 7 of 7

FINAL VALUATION

The residence described herein can be compared to the finest houses that have been built in the Nita City area. Modernizations and improvements have been made throughout the years.

With the exceptions of a few larger residences such as the one noted as No. 5 above, most of the homes in the surrounding one quarter mile from the Easterfield residence are smaller and are valued at lower amounts. The other houses noted in the Market Data Approach are from the Waverly neighborhood within a mile from the Easterfield home where all the houses are comparable to the Easterfield home. The Easterfield home has amenities they lack and is closer to the lake and to rail transportation to the business district, making the market approach somewhat more speculative. The area around the Easterfield home is also more culturally and racially diverse than the Waverly neighborhood, and I feel, more attractive for that reason. A home identical to the Easterfield home would sell for $1.5 million in Waverly.

Therefore, after taking into consideration the values indicated by both the cost and market approaches, and after careful consideration of those pertinent factors affecting the value of the property herein described, it is my opinion that the fair market value of the Easterfield property on December 18, 2002 assuming good title and disregarding any liens or other encumbrances (including unpaid general taxes or special assessments which may exist) is:

ONE MILLION ONE HUNDRED FIFTY THOUSAND DOLLARS ($1,150,000)

Respectfully submitted,

George Peters

George R. Peters

JOHN KRAUS OPINION LETTER
Page 1 of 3

January 12, 2003

Brian Moehn
Berry, Moehn, Foley & Madden, P.C.
Suite 1120, First National Bank Bldg.
Nita City, Nita

Dear Mr. Moehn:

I have reviewed the Appraisal of Real Estate submitted by Mr. George Peters for the Peters, George and Lintel firm. You have asked me to analyze the methods and conclusions of Mr. Peters, but not to conduct my own independent appraisal of the Easterfield property. In this I have done what I was told to do by your office and I offer no independent appraisal. I have not visited the property myself nor conducted any independent research.

As you know, I have known Mr. George Peters for quite some time. From 1984 to 1989 I worked for Darius Realty as a real estate broker. Mr. Peters was my immediate superior during that time and introduced me to the world of real estate valuation and sales. In 1989 I left Darius to get my M.B.A. in Accountancy and have taught part time in the business school at Nita University since that time. I have not done any appraisals myself since I left Darius. I would not say that my relationship with Peters was good, and I should say that my decision to move to an accounting firm was motivated in part by my distaste for the somewhat cynical methods and style that Darius represented and for which Peters had something of a reputation. One of the aspects of Peters' reputation in the real estate community was as someone who manipulated his work as an appraiser to the needs of the situation at hand.

It seems to me that Mr. Peters has done what his customer, the firm representing plaintiff, wanted, but in the process has neglected the most basic standards of any real estate valuation that at least aspires to be a somewhat objective science.

Real estate appraisal is necessarily an enterprise that requires a degree of judgment. Reasonable people may differ. I believe however that the report submitted by Mr. Peters is simply beyond the pale. It illustrates the kind of willfulness that led me to leave the field before I could be required to compromise my independent judgment in the interests of the client's position. It is true that I have myself not conducted a real estate appraisal since I left the firm in 1989, but I think I know a compromised piece of work when I see it.

JOHN KRAUS OPINION LETTER
Page 2 of 3

First some basics as to the method and concepts in valuation. The concept of "market value" is something of a theoretical construct. It seeks to identify the highest price that a property will bring if exposed for sale in the open market allowing a very indefinite "reasonable time" to find a (hypothetical) purchaser who buys with the (full) knowledge of all the uses to which the property is adapted or for which it is capable of being used. Of course no such buyer ever actually exists.

The method on which Peters places the most reliance in his analysis is the cost approach. His argument for doing that is that the market approach is rather more speculative because of the paucity of comparables to the Easterfield home in his immediate area. At its best, the cost approach is very much a highly conventional, artificial method for determining market value, which is why, in my view it should, except in extraordinary circumstances, be subordinated to the market approach. In the cost approach the appraiser estimates the cost of building a new building at today's construction costs and then depreciates that (hypothetical) building to reach a valuation of the real building. It is true that the cost approach is universally used throughout the industry and important business and personal decisions are made using it all the time. It is also true that any competent appraiser would be remiss not to rely in part on this approach. The method is taught in courses in valuation in all business schools, including our school. The cost approach in Peters' hands is, however, an exercise somewhere between guess and wishful thinking. It is true that reproduction costs of luxury housing of the sort that the Easterfields own can reach as high as $200 per square foot, though for that reason very little of it is being built in the Nita area. However, given the age and condition of the house I should think that the depreciation figures are very much underestimated and that something in the order of 70 percent might be more realistic. One can easily see from the very round numbers that Peter uses (50 percent and $1,000 per square foot for the land) that he is aiming at a predetermined figure. I look forward to explaining the forms of depreciation and my views as to why Peters has underestimated their effects when we meet next week.

I do not dispute Peters' contention that a home identical to the Easterfield home, which does have some distinctive features, might sell for over $1 million in the Waverly area, though the comparables that Peters produces certainly do not support that conclusion. Easterfield's home is not, however, in that area. Most of the homes in the area surrounding the Easterfield home are much smaller and are valued at amounts quite a bit lower. Peters suggests that the "cultural and racial diversity" that results from this mix translates into an advantage from a valuation perspective. This "feeling" on which Peters relies is counterintuitive and not consistent with my own experience. Most persons who invest over a million dollars in a home prefer to live in neighborhoods where most homes are similarly valued.

Peters never gives us the formula by which the market data he reports affected his final evaluation. Since the cost approach in his hands indicates a valuation of approximately $1.3 million and his actual valuation is lower, I expect that he used it simply to lower the cost approach valuation in an extremely intuitive sort of way. The only home in the immediate area of the Easterfield house is the comparable at 389 Rolling Hills Lane. The home has the same number of rooms as the Easterfield home, one fewer bedroom, the same number of stories, and is of the same style and is on the market for $200,000 less than the Easterfield home. Even at that price there have been no offers. (It is not unusual for homes in this bracket, where demand is often quite intermittent and

JOHN KRAUS OPINION LETTER
Page 3 of 3

inelastic, to be on the market at prices as much as 20 percent over the actual selling price.) Comparable number 3 is also a Norman home with one fewer rooms and one fewer bedroom, admittedly on a much smaller lot (the actual area is not given in Peters' report and I have followed your instructions in not doing my own research beyond the report), but it is in the Waverly area and it sold for only $620,000 just recently. Comparable number 4 is a much newer home with two fewer rooms, only one fewer bedrooms, more baths, on a large lot and it sold for $720,000. The other comparables do not support Peters' valuation.

Two quibbles. There is an addition error in the square foot calculations for the house. The total should be 12,680 feet. This throws off the rest of the cost approach calculations somewhat. And the fixtures in the upstairs bedroom are not gold! Mr. Easterfield tells me they are brass.

I hope this preliminary analysis is adequate and is what you wanted. Should you require my services further, my hourly rate will continue to be $110.00. I enclose a bill for $880.00 for work done to date. I expect that the additional time necessary for me to testify would be ten more hours for my own preparation in addition to the time you would wish to spend with me and the time it would take actually to testify at trial.

Sincerely,

John Kraus

Section Nine—Opening Statements

PROBLEM 57.   OPENING STATEMENT   (MacIntyre v. Easterfield)

A. For the plaintiff in *MacIntyre v. Easterfield*, present a ten-minute segment from your opening statement.

B. For the defendant in MacIntyre v. Easterfield, present a ten-minute segment from your opening statement.

—Do not attempt to squeeze an entire opening statement into ten minutes. Concentrate on presenting a theory of the case and supporting it with the facts that you intend to prove. You need not present the beginning part of the opening statement; any ten-minute segment is acceptable.

PROBLEM 58.   OPENING STATEMENT   (State v. Mitchell)

A. For the prosecution in *State v. Mitchell*, present a ten-minute segment from your opening statement.

B. For the defense in *State v. Mitchell*, present a ten-minute segment from your opening statement.

—Do not attempt to squeeze an entire opening statement into ten minutes. Concentrate on presenting a theory of the case and supporting it with the facts that you intend to prove. You need not present the beginning part of the opening statement; any ten-minute segment is acceptable.

SECTION TEN—FINAL ARGUMENTS

PROBLEM 59.   FINAL ARGUMENT   (*MacIntyre v. Easterfield*)

Part One

A.   For the plaintiff in *MacIntyre v. Easterfield*, present a ten-minute argument-in-chief (final argument) on the issue of liability.

B.   For the defendant in *MacIntyre v. Easterfield*, present a ten-minute argument-in-chief (final argument) on the issue of liability.

C.   For the plaintiff, present five minutes of rebuttal.

—Do not attempt to squeeze an entire final argument into ten minutes. Concentrate on presenting a theory of the case. You need not present the beginning part of the opening statement; any ten-minute segment is acceptable. (Plaintiff, however, may only use rebuttal to respond to the defendant's argument.)

Part Two

A.   For the plaintiff, present a ten-minute segment of final argument limited to a discussion of the credibility of one or more witnesses.

B.   For the defendant, present a ten-minute segment of final argument limited to a discussion of the credibility of one or more witnesses.

C.   For the plaintiff, present five minutes of rebuttal.

Part Three

A.   For the plaintiff, present ten minutes of final argument on the issue of damages.

B.   For the defendant, present ten minutes of final argument on the issue of damages.

C.   For the plaintiff, present five minutes of rebuttal.

PROBLEM 60.   FINAL ARGUMENT   (*State v. Mitchell*)

Part One

A.   For the prosecution in *State v. Mitchell*, present ten minutes of argument-in-chief (final argument).

B.   For the defense in *State v. Mitchell*, present ten minutes of argument-in-chief (final argument).

—Do not attempt to squeeze an entire final argument into ten minutes. Concentrate on presenting a theory of the case. Any ten-minute segment is acceptable; you need not present the beginning part of the final argument. (The prosecution, however, may only use rebuttal to respond to the defense argument.)

C.   For the prosecution, present five minutes of rebuttal.

Part Two

A. For the prosecution, present a ten-minute segment of final argument limited to a discussion of the credibility of one or more witnesses.

B. For the defense, present a ten-minute segment of final argument limited to a discussion of the credibility of one or more witnesses.

C. For the prosecution, present five minutes of rebuttal.

Part Three

A. For the prosecution, present ten minutes of final argument on Joe Mitchell's alibi.

B. For the defense, present ten minutes of final argument on Joe Mitchell's alibi.

C. For the prosecution, present five minutes of rebuttal.

Part Four

A. For the prosecution, present ten minutes of final argument on the issue of motive.

B. For the defense, present ten minutes of final argument on the issue of motive.

C. For the prosecution, present five minutes of rebuttal.

SECTION ELEVEN—JURY SELECTION

PROBLEM 61.   JURY SELECTION   (*MacIntyre v. Easterfield*)

A. For the plaintiff, conduct voir dire examination on behalf of your client.

B. For the defendant, conduct voir dire examination on behalf of your client.

—Be prepared to discuss any possible peremptory strikes or challenges for cause.

PROBLEM 62.   JURY SELECTION   (*State v. Mitchell*)

A. For the prosecution, conduct voir dire examination on behalf of the state.

B. For the defense, conduct voir dire examination on behalf of your client.

—Be prepared to discuss any possible peremptory strikes or challenges for cause.